The
First
Catch
Seafood
Cookbook

Happy Reading

We had a great
time eating.

Halifax
1996

J Baldwin

The Fine Catch Seafood Cookbook

Julie V. Watson

RAGWEED
THE ISLAND PUBLISHER

Cover photograph:
Barrett & MacKay Photographers

Printed and bound in Canada by:
Webcom

Published by:
Ragweed Press
P.O. Box 2023
Charlottetown, P.E.I.
Canada, C1A 7N7

Distributors:
Canada: General Distribution Services
United States: Inland Book Company
United Kingdom: Turnaround Distribution

Canadian Cataloguing in Publication Data

Watson, Julie V., 1943-

The fine catch seafood cookbook

Includes index.
ISBN 0-921556-45-4

1. Cookery (Seafood)   I. Title.

TX747.W37 1994   641.6'92   C94-950060-7

*Special thanks to all of the great chefs and
cooks who shared their recipes with me,
making my preparation of this book a joy.*

Acknowledgments

When I began trying to list all of those individuals I would like to thank for this book, the pages rapidly filled, and I was forced to shorten the acknowledgements which appear here. Instead, my thanks go out to all of those individuals mentioned throughout the book — the chefs and restaurateurs, the friends, everyone who shared their expertise. Most of your names appear with the recipes.

Special thanks also go to:

Jack Watson, my husband, who rarely complains about the long hours I spend on projects such as this; Paul Prudhomme, whose encouragement means so much; Kasey Wilson, who helps when I need it, especially with moral support; Alan Baker, who gave me the opportunity to work with and learn about lobster; Dave Younker at P.E.I. Fisheries for his ongoing support; our special friends Deb and Tim, Beth and David, Helen and Roy, Carol and Russ; and, especially, the editors and writers at the many food magazines which I consider to be my bibles, particularly those at *Simply Seafood* — a truly fine publication — *Eating Well* and *Canadian Living*.

Contents

Introduction

Seafood. It's the section on a menu to which my eyes turn first. It's what I most often think of when planning a meal. My fascination with it is reflected in the hundreds of recipes and cookbooks I gather wherever I travel. There is nothing more appealing to me than a good feed of lobster prepared in one of a dozen favourite ways, or scallops in a rich cheese sauce, or mussels, straight from the steaming pot. In my family, we love fish. We delight in trying new species, as well as old favourites prepared in new ways.

Living as we do in the coastal province of Prince Edward Island, Canada, we are in close contact with the seafood industry. Here we have access to dozens of locally harvested fish and shellfish: lobster, mussels, oysters, clams, trout, mackerel, cod and crab, just to name a few. Modern handling and shipping methods mean we also have access to many seafoods from "away": shark, salmon, catfish, monkfish and dozens more. When we travel, we seek out species unique to their areas.

For my husband and me, seafood is often a pivot around which vacations spin. We love to travel, to experience the cuisine and the ambiance of a place. And by "cuisine" I don't mean the offerings of fancy, high priced restaurants, although we love those as well. We travel as we live — on a tight budget! Most of our favourite meals have been enjoyed over campfires, in little diners, at someone's cottage or even at affairs where one samples dishes prepared by many skilled hands — church suppers, receptions and the more lavish gatherings of chefs who each offer up samples of their specialty.

We had one memorable feast cooking salmon fillets on our Coleman stove in a roadside picnic area in Washington State as a dust storm raged around us. Four picnic tables were arranged under a roof shaped a little like a clover leaf — each was private, yet in close proximity to the rest; two were sheltered from the wind. While we cooked up a feast of mushrooms, broccoli, new potatoes and salmon purchased earlier that day at Pike's Market in Seattle, volunteers gathered at the next table to serve coffee to travellers as a fundraiser for their local ambulance program. People pulled off the road to wait out the storm, and we chatted, talked, accepted accolades about our cooking prowess and had a thoroughly good time as the wind blew tumbleweeds past and dust encapsulated us in a small world.

Another memorable feast was our first real lobster feed in Nova Scotia. What seemed like huge numbers of lobster, fresh from the boat, were boiled up outside in a huge pot rigged over a propane burner. The table inside was covered with layer upon layer of newspaper. A chopping block with a big chipped cleaver was placed in the middle. Rolls of paper towels were situated here and there, along with a few condiments, including vinegar, a mixture of mayonnaise and mustard, and melted butter. The lobsters were brought in and a pile dumped within arm's reach of every seat. "Dig in folks," encouraged our hostess. And dig in we did. It didn't take us long to learn the method of eating lobster favoured in that Nova Scotia community — eating with the hands God gave us and the occasional whack with a cleaver.

Then there was the time we went cod jigging here in P.E.I. We took our catch back to the campground and fed everyone who strolled by. And the same thing happened with clams. We dug more than our fill, and then, not knowing what to do with them, offered them to others in the campground. A group of folks from Quebec cooked up a number of dishes and asked us to their campsite to share them — and that's when I really started collecting recipes.

I'm also one of those people who really do remember eating fish and chips brought home wrapped in newspapers. In fact, many of my fondest memories from my childhood in England centre around food. My Dad, after all, was a baker and my Mom worked right by his side. When we emigrated to Canada, Mom worked in a fish and chip store. I still drool at the thought of Charlie Hunt's halibut, deep fried in batter and served up with a good strong malt vinegar. My first dates used to end up at the fish and chip shop, where I would wait for Mom to get off work. I would put my nickels in the juke box, listen to Tommy Sands and Elvis, drink cherry cokes and feast on fish and chips. I even loved leftover fish eaten cold. Mom would wrap them up and bring them home to warm in the oven — if I didn't get them first.

In all the years I've been eating seafood I only once had a dish I could not eat. It was an oily fish and, I suspect, very badly prepared. It was the memory of that one dish that turned my interest to seafood cooking. Why, I wondered, was it so bad and others so good? I never did figure out what made that one dish bad. But I certainly did figure out many of the secrets great cooks use to make the thousands of other really good seafood dishes. Those secrets are, to a great degree, shared with you in the pages that follow.

The first section of this book contains general know-how about seafood, and I really recommend that you read it. The general knowledge, as well as information specific to different species, is helpful when buying and storing. Basic cooking techniques are included and are often sufficient to prepare a meal without going to a more complicated recipe. The sections of the book that follow the general section contain recipes that transcend borders — they come from many sources and reflect trends not only in North America, but worldwide.

Indeed, more than ever before, North America has become a melting pot of cultures. As more and more peoples are represented by our population, the demand for new, different and often very unusual foods has increased. The result is a conundrum for those trying to define Canadian or even North American cuisine. It is, in fact, a synthesis of countless other ethnic cuisines. The recent profusion of ethnic res-taurants is incredibly exciting. New foods are developing as different cultures assimilate surrounding ethnic influences. The blending of these individual elements of distinct styles of cuisine has even been given a name: "fusion" cooking. The dictionary defines "fuse" as "to blend or bring together by or as if by melting." Fusion cooking, both literally and figuratively, reflects the rapid changes taking place in kitchens today.

The changes start at the professional level. Chefs no longer feel constrained by formal disciplines of cooking. They are venturing towards new taste sensations and non-traditional methods of food preparation. In turn, those of us who sample their dishes are also becoming much bolder and taking charge of our own kitchens in a different way than ever before. When the trend towards healthy living was added to the ethnic melting pot, we suddenly discovered even more exciting additions to our cooking repertoire. It is quite common to see households enjoy Thai dishes one night, Southwest or Tex Mex the next, and then a good old-fashioned down east seafood stew. The common link today is our ongoing desire to have our food intake reflect less than 30% fat. We haven't given up rich cream chowders, or sauces, or deep-frying, but we are tempering our consumption and accepting that the occasional treat is not catastrophic if we eat in a healthy way as a general habit.

All of these trends are reflected in the following pages. You will find the rich and decadent alongside the low-fat and nutritionally sound. Where possible, I have taken the healthy route.

Other, sometimes ominous, trends are affecting what we eat. Changing world markets bring more and more foods to our door, and consequently the variety of fresh seafood has increased. However, even as this is happening, the fisheries themselves are experiencing radical change. Many species are suffering from poor management and have become scarce, or waters have become polluted, making the harvesting of shellfish and sometimes fish unviable. Fortunately, in Canada, our waters are tested regularly so we are ensured of a safe supply of seafood. We also have a booming aquaculture, or fish farming, industry. And some species, such as Canadian lobster have been well-managed and are in plentiful supply.

So, in addition to reflecting food preparation trends, the pages of this book reflect the availability of seafoods. There are more recipes for seafoods such as salmon, lobster, mussels and shrimp than for some other, less readily available, species. It is important to remember, too, that some of our best products have not yet found their way into the seafood outlets. Typical of this situation is frozen lobster meat. Packed in an 11.3 oz/320 g can and flash frozen, it is perfect for many dishes, yet hard to find outside of Atlantic Canada. I urge consumers to ask for these products, particularly those that are from properly managed fisheries or aquafarming operations.

Many of the recipes in these pages are ones my husband and I have discovered in our travels. We count ourselves very lucky to have met so many good cooks and food aficionados. Much of the "how-to" information comes from friends in the seafood writing and cooking business. The recipes come from chefs, teachers and home cooks. I am fortunate enough to have found a small place in a fraternity of food lovers that ranges the world. As a result many, many cultures and nationalities are represented here.

Indeed, as I worked on this cookbook, I came to feel that I've been blessed. So many people have shared their concepts and cooking techniques with me — and now I am able to share them with others. I've gathered my favourites together in these pages, and I believe that the variety of dishes offered is what makes this book unique.

Most of all, I hope you enjoy reading my collection and sampling many of the wonderful recipes that follow. Enjoy!

Julie Watson

Seafood Know-How

This chapter presents basic information: which species are fat and which are lean, how to buy and store seafood and cooking information. Remember: new technology is making it possible for all of us to have access to excellent seafood.

World Trends in Seafood

H ere in North America there are very definite trends towards healthier eating, resulting in an increased popularity for seafood. I believe that those who are impelled to try seafood because it's good for them find that they like what they are eating, and are swelling the ranks of seafood lovers. The result is more variety, better methods of presentation in restaurants and higher quality products at seafood counters.

Another trend, that towards food safety, has forced the marketplace to provide higher quality product than ever before. Canada has installed an enviable set of regulations for the handling and processing of all fisheries products. Other countries are quickly following suit. You, the consumer, must direct this trend to keep it on track. Demand high quality. Learn how to distinguish a good fresh product. And, please, take advantage of the wonderful frozen products on the market today. If your grocery store doesn't stock quality frozen lobster, shrimp, crab and a variety of fish, ask for these products — and keep asking until they are put on the shelves. They are frozen quickly and safely and are very convenient to use.

The third trend in North American seafood cuisine is an expansion of our culinary horizons. Call it "fusion cuisine," a world melting pot or whatever you like. The truth is that we North Americans are becoming enthralled with the tastes and sensations of our global neighbours and becoming much more daring in what we eat. This book is designed to introduce some of those new cuisines in recipes you can prepare at home.

When I began to write *A Fine Catch*, I intended to include a factual section on world trends not only in seafood cuisine, but in the fishery. It didn't take me long to realize that the real trend is rapid change, and this is the factor that makes it a very difficult task to categorically describe the world fishery. For example, five years ago shrimp were a luxury product we enjoyed only when we left our Island home. The only ones we could buy in local shops were in tins, or were so limp from travel and age that they had no flavour. Today we can walk into a grocery store and buy frozen shrimp in many forms. These shrimp are fast frozen within a short time of being harvested, and they are delicious. Even as I gloat over this ready supply, I hear from the experts that supplies will soon drop off and prices will rise because of a disease or virus popping up in the warm-water aquafarming operations. Shrimp will still be available, but there may be less of them for a while.

Aquaculture is a wonderful development which has put readily available, high quality fish and shellfish into consumers' hands. It is responsible for the excellent salmon widely available today. Trout, Arctic Char, shrimp, catfish, crawfish, even halibut, are farmed. And, of course, the oyster and mussel farming industry has made Prince Edward Island, in particular, famous all over the world. On P.E.I., we have added clam and scallop farming to our aquaculture enterprises, and others will surely follow. Similar progress is found in aquafarming operations around the world. But the system isn't flawless. Like all farming operations, there are good times and bad. Overcrowding can cause problems, and if a problem does occur, it can wipe out an entire catch. These are natural occurrences, often caused by factors such as water temperature, plankton blooms, disease and virus. Safeguards like vaccines are being developed to ward off disease.

I personally have great faith in the future of aquafarming. New technology, increased knowledge and greater experience will lead the way to even bigger success in the future. The recipes within the pages of this book lean towards farmed species, such as salmon and mussels, and towards fisheries that are well managed, such as the lobster fishery. I believe very strongly that we must learn to respect the natural wild stocks, allowing them time to regenerate. We must stop destructive fishing practices and learn to handle catches in ways that ensure high quality, safe products.

Even those steps, however, are sometimes not enough. Canada has some of the highest quality standards in the world, and we monitor what is happening within our waters very carefully, yet today there is a moratorium on Canadian cod fishing off the Atlantic coast. The stock, it appears, is gone. Those who understand the industry as a whole warn that even if the cod come back, the fishery will never support the same number of jobs as it did in the past. The reason for this has to do with the supply of cod on the world market — to compete in the consumer marketplace, we would have to sell our catch so cheaply it would hardly pay fishers a decent day's wage.

The key, I believe, is an acceptance by all citizens that our actions have ramifications far beyond what we ourselves can readily see. Perhaps we need to ban the very things that make our fishery efficient today. For example, with our "high tech" methods of finding and scooping up whole schools of fish, we can easily wipe out breeding stock.

The world is changing, and changing very rapidly. That means that some species are being over-fished and will become rare in the marketplace. When they are available, they will be very highly priced. On the other hand, well-managed fisheries actually catch more than they can sell. The Canadian lobster industry, for example, regulates harvest by season and by size. The result is a steady supply which in fact exceeds demand. Their problem is one of getting the catch to the consumer! And then there are the farmed species — mussels, catfish, shrimp and craw-fish are very successful in eastern North America. Other species do equally as well in other areas of the world.

If you want to check out world trends in the fishery this month, talk to your fishmonger. He or she will tell you what is available and what is not. Or turn to seafood and food magazines — because they are publish-ed monthly, they are able to keep up with the trends.

And always remember that it doesn't really matter what the trend is. Choose seafood from what is available to you in your town. Then choose a healthy method of cooking that you and your family and friends will enjoy. You'll be right on track with the most important trend: your own.

Shopping Wisely

In an effort to provide maximum value and freshness, fish and shellfish are transported very quickly from the water to the consumer. How-ever, in order to find the best product, you as the consumer must also shop wisely. It is most important to know where your seafood comes from. Try to establish a good rapport with your seafood seller. If they know you as a regular customer they will treat you well. Also, use your common sense. Look at the place selling seafood. If it is dirty, if the coolers have ice build-up, if ice in displays is melting away, or if seafood is left at room temperature, then move on. Find a well-run outlet. If you are uncertain of the fresh product, then don't hesitate to turn to frozen. The quality of frozen seafood is often hard to beat unless you live near a fishing port. Check the individual seafood listings in this book for tips unique to buying, storing and cooking particular species.

Here are some tests professionals use to ensure that they are getting the best possible quality seafood. Apply as many of the following checks as you can. They are listed in their approximate order of importance:

1. Smell the fish. It should have a fresh, clean, "sea" aroma. Very strong odours are a clear indication that the fish is aging or was improperly handled or stored.

2. Feel the skin. The skin should feel slick and moist. Scales, if any, should be firmly attached.

3. Look at the fins and tail. They should be moist, fresh, flexible and full, and should not appear ragged or dry.

4. Press the flesh. It should feel firm and elastic; if there is a visible finger imprint, the fish is not fresh.

5. Check the eyes. The eyes should be clear and full. As the fish ages, the eyes will begin to lose moisture and sink back into the head.

6. Check the gills. They should have a good red to maroon colour, with no evidence of greying or browning, and should be moist and fresh-looking.

7. Check the belly. There should be no sign of "belly burn," which occurs when the guts are not removed promptly — the stomach enzymes begin to eat the flesh, causing it to come away from the bones. There should also be no breaks or tears in the flesh.

8. Check live shellfish for signs of movement. Lobster and crab should move about. Clams, wild mussels and oysters should be tightly closed. As they age, they will start to open. Bags containing many open shells are old, and should be rejected. Any shells that do not snap shut when tapped should be discarded — the shellfish are dead. Cultured mussels are another matter. Because they have been grown in ideal conditions they tend to be a bit laid back and it is quite common for them to lay around with their shells gaping open a little. Use the tap test. If they don't close when sharply tapped, and also look dried or unhealthy, discard them. Canadian Cultured Mussels all go to the seafood dealer tagged with the date they were harvested. If in doubt, ask to see the tag.

Fish

I t is very easy to overcook fish. People more familiar with cooking meat may tend to cook fish too long. For perfectly cooked fish, we suggest the following guidelines combined with the check mentioned below. If following a recipe, use the directions; however, remember that experience will also teach you about your stove's temperature ranges, which types of fish cook faster and so on.

Buying:

There are several terms used to refer to how fish are prepared for sale. Shopping will be simpler if you know them:

Drawn fish: A whole fish minus the internal organs.

Dressed fish: A fish with the internal organs removed (eviscerated) as well as the head, tail and fins removed. If you are buying a small fish, such as a trout, you may see them referred to as "pan dressed," meaning they are ready for the pan.

Fish steak: A crosscut slice (usually ½ to 1 inch/1.25 to 2.5 cm thick) from a large dressed fish.

Fish fillet: A piece of the fish cut lengthwise from the sides, and away from the backbone. These are usually boneless and often have the skin removed.

Storing:

Purchase seafood as close to cooking time as possible — the day it is to be used is ideal, or one day ahead. Under proper storage conditions, fish and shellfish can be stored in the refrigerator for several days without losing their quality. My recommendation is to take some tips from restaurants or seafood retailers, who use the following methods of storage:

Whole Fish —

1. Whole fish should be cleaned and dressed. It can be rinsed as soon as you obtain it, particularly the cavity. However, scaling and boning should be left until preparing to cook.

2. Whole fish are best placed on a bed of shaved or flaked ice in a perforated container of stainless steel or plastic. The fish should be belly down, and the cavity can be filled with shaved ice as well. If you have several fish, then layer with shaved ice.

3. Put the perforated container inside a large second container so that the water will drain away as the ice melts. Fish should not be left sitting in a pool of water. Shaved or flaked ice is preferable for storing, because the water can drain away more quickly, keeping the fish dry and avoiding bruising of the flesh. Fish should be thoroughly drained and iced down fresh every day.

Fillets or Steaks —

Store these in a plastic container, set them on or in ice, or put them in the coldest part of your refrigerator. Do not set fillets or steaks directly on ice. Much of the flavour will be rinsed away as the ice melts, and loss of texture may also result.

Frozen Fish —

Should be kept at 0°F/-18°C until ready to thaw and cook. Do not accept any frozen fish with white frost along the edges. This indicates freezer burn, the result of improper packaging, or thawing and refreezing.

Cooking:

Fish can be cooked in numerous ways that range from simple to complex. As one of the most delicate foods, fish does need some attention as to how it is cooked. It cooks quickly with a minimum of preparation, and care must be taken not to overcook, or to cook too far in advance, as this can cause dryness and toughness. The best way to prevent this is to become familiar with the colour change fish undergoes during cooking. Raw fish has a watery, translucent look, while cooked fish takes on an opaque, whitish tint. When this colour change occurs at the centre of the thickest part of the fish, it is done. Successful meals featuring fish simply require a little planning so that the fish will be cooked at the same time as other foods.

Actual cooking times depend on your stove or oven setting and the temperature and texture of the fish. If you are uncertain about a new fish, ask your fishmonger or retailer for information about it. Most of them carry recipes and cooking instructions and can at least tell you the species of a fish and whether it is fat or lean.

Broiling, poaching and micro-cooking are healthy and simple preparation methods — ideal for fish. Generally speaking, follow the directions in your recipe. Please note, however, that poached or broiled fish, by far the healthiest presentations, can be teamed with sauces and salsas for wonderful easy meals. We have included instructions for these, along with a few other cooking tips below.

Basic Cooking Guidelines:

- Fresh fillets and steaks should be broiled, grilled, baked or poached 4 to 6 minutes for each ½ inch/1.25 cm of thickness.

- The same guideline can be applied to whole dressed fish; or, when baking or poaching, allow 6 to 9 minutes for every ½ lb/250 g.

- When using frozen fish, follow the package instructions, or thaw completely and use those above.

Poaching — Poaching is the healthiest and least fattening method of cooking, in that no oil or sauce is cooked with the fish. Barely cover the fish with liquid and simmer 10 minutes per 1 inch/2.5 cm thickness. Save stock to make sauces, chowders, etc.

Poaching is as easy as boiling water, according to many experts. All you do is cook fish in an almost-boiling liquid such as wine, beer, broth, milk or flavoured water. You can poach whole drawn or dressed fish, steaks, fillets or chunks cut from a large fish like salmon (cut across like you would a super thick steak). Usually fish is poached on a stovetop, although it can also be poached in the oven or a microwave.

Select cooking utensil (skillet, stove-top glassware, roasting pan or oblong fish poacher) large enough to hold fish. Add poaching liquid with herbs or vegetable seasonings, if desired, and bring to slow boil (small bubbles just beginning to break the surface). Poaching liquid should just cover fish. Add fish and simmer, covered, just below boiling point, until fish is done. Allow 4 to 6 minutes per ½ inch/1.25 cm thickness and test with fork to ensure that it is done.

Frozen fish will require as much as 6 to 9 minutes per ½ inch/1.25 cm. Temperature is vital when poaching fish. Keep poaching liquid around 175°F/90°C, just below boiling (boiling will flake the fish apart).

An electric frying pan is ideal for poaching fish because of its depth, shape and easily controlled temperature. The poaching liquid can easily be made into a sauce by straining out vegetables, then simmering liquid to reduce or thicken it.

Broiling — Nothing is easier than broiling fish steaks or fillets. The secret to ensuring moistness is to brush fish occasionally while broiling with oil, a marinade, or even melted butter. Fish cooks so quickly that portions less than 1 inch/2.5 cm thick need never be turned. Not turning also prevents breakage.

Place fish 6 to 8 inches/15 to 20 cm from heat and place water in the bottom of broiling pan to keep fish moist.

Deep-frying — Pat fish dry with paper towelling, then fry fish in vegetable oil heated to 375°F/190°C. At this temperature, a crust forms almost immediately, holding in juices and preventing fat from soaking in.

Pan-frying — When pan-frying fish, use breading rather than batter, as low heat causes batter coating to become soggy. Heat oil over medium high heat. Slide in fish and cook until ready to carefully turn. Do not overcook.

Grilling or Barbecuing — A natural for fish, because it seals in flavour and moistness, just as broiling does. Grilling also requires the use of a marinade, oil or butter to keep the fish moist and prevent sticking. See the chapter on grilling for more information.

Marinating — A marinade serves two purposes: it enhances taste and adds moisture (without adding many calories). Fresh or frozen fish should be marinated in the refrigerator, with the fish turned often to ensure even absorption of the marinade and flavours. If using frozen fish, allow extra time so that the fish will at least partially thaw and thus be able to absorb the flavour. The longer the fish marinates, the more flavour it absorbs. Lean, delicate fish absorb a strongly flavoured marinade in 15 minutes; milder flavours can take up to 1 hour to be absorbed. Don't marinate delicate fish longer than 15 minutes in marinades with a lemon, lime or orange juice base. The acid in citrus juice can "cook" the fish.

An easy way to marinate fish is to prepare the marinade in a heavy or double-thickness plastic bag and add the fish. Close the bag tight and place it in a shallow bowl in case it leaks. Turn 3 to 4 times. See the chapter on grilling for more marinating information.

Testing Fish for Doneness:

To test that your fish is cooked, place the tines of a table fork into the flesh at a 45-degree angle. Gently twist and pull out some of the fish. It will flake easily if it is properly cooked. If the flesh resists flaking, then the fish is not done. If it is mealy, dry or tough, it is overdone. You can also tell whether fish is done by the appearance of the flesh. Carefully separate flakes so that you can see into the centre of your fillet or steak. If the centre line is translucent, it is not cooked. Cooked fish is opaque. Firm-fleshed fish such as halibut or swordfish does not flake as easily as softer fleshed ones such as cod. Rely on the visual check to test for doneness.

Serving Whole Fish:

When whole fish is poached or baked with its skin on, you can remove the skin and bone before taking it to the table. Cut along the centre of the backbone, drawing your knife from head to tail.

Use a knife and fork or spoon and loosen then carefully pull the skin towards the stomach. It will easily peel off; discard it.

Carefully lift the top piece of fish away from the backbone using a fork, pie lifter or egg flipper, depending on the size of the fish. If you are careful, you should be able to do this without breaking the fish. If you do break it, you can fit it back together to serve.

Using a fork, raise the backbone and pull it away with your fingers. Discard it. The bottom half of the fish is now exposed. You can place the top portion back on, or arrange it nicely on a serving plate and remove the bottom from the skin and add it.

A little practice and you will become quite proficient at this operation. It is well worth the effort when you serve a luscious whole salmon, and its delightful orange flesh becomes the centre of an attractive presentation.

Fish Facts:

Fish fall into two categories: lean and fat. With so many new species making their way to seafood retailers, it has become rather difficult to know which is which, and what to do with them.

Lean fish have less than 5 percent fat. They poach well because the liquid used in poaching keeps them from drying out. If you bake, broil, microwave or grill them, you will probably want to brush them with butter or margarine, or serve with a sauce or even lemon juice squeezed over top to replenish the moisture lost in cooking.

Saying that a fish is fat does not imply that it is not good for you. In fact fish, whether canned, fresh or frozen, is packed with health and nutritional benefits. It is normally low in fat and calories compared to, say, red meat. And the oils in fish, called Omega-3 fatty acids, have lots of health advantages. All fish, even shellfish, have some of these good oils, but the fish richest in them are the fattier varieties. A sensible dietary consideration would be to alternate the types of fish you eat so that you get the benefits of both types, but keep control of your fat intake. See the list which follows for examples of lean and fat seafood:

Bass—lean: sweet tasting and light, as long as skin is not cooked or eaten.

Bluefish—fat: chewy with firm, moist flesh that is grey in colour. Generally not good for poaching or chowder because of its texture and oil content.

Black Cod—fat: a.k.a. Alaskan black cod, butterfish and sablefish. In Chinese markets this fish can be found cured or smoked and often dyed bright yellow or red. These versions are usually too salty for North American taste. Fresh black cod is described as luxurious, velvety and rich. The taste is sweet, but mild. An oily fish, and very versatile.

Butterfish—fat: slightly oily taste and soft texture (see Black Cod).

Carp—lean

Catfish—lean: successfully farmed and rapidly becoming very popular. Firm when cooked, yet tender and delicate. Perfect in salads, chowders and stews as it doesn't flake apart. Usually inexpensive.

Cod—lean: very versatile; has a tender flesh with mild flavour.

Croaker — lean: white-fleshed.

Cusk — lean: white-fleshed, with a mild taste. Similar to haddock. Good in chowders and takes well to seasonings and sauces.

Eel — fat: smoked eel is a delicious appetizer and a rich fish which should be eaten within one day; is purchased live or fresh.

Flounder — lean: see sole.

Grouper — lean: thick, firm flesh. Large steaks are best broiled to keep them moist. Also good baked in a sauce, fried, or poached in soups and stews.

Haddock — lean: white tender flesh, high in protein, low in fat. Versatile.

Hake — lean: there at least a dozen species of this member of the cod family, which is also known as "whiting" in some areas of the world. The flesh is snow-white, sweet and delicate, although somewhat less bland in flavour than cod. It has a slightly higher oil content, and thus a softer flesh, necessitating careful handling in cooking and storage. It can be used successfully in most recipes designed for cod or haddock.

Halibut — lean: delicate, slightly sweet flavour, with snow-white flesh and succulent, firm texture which allow it to maintain its shape and tender flake during cooking. Very versatile; good hot or cold.

Herring — fat: very bony, so best used as fillets no longer than 5 inches long and cooked over a high heat. Smoked herring is very good.

Mackerel — fat: firm texture with a distinct flavour. Tends to lose flavour quickly when not iced or refrigerated, so eat fresh. Freezes well.

Marlin — lean: marinate, as it dries quickly in cooking. Can be used as substitute for swordfish, tuna and shark.

Monkfish — lean: also known as the angler, sea devil, goosefish and lotte, this ugly fish is low-fat and firm-textured, and has a mild, sweet flavour that has been compared to lobster. In fact, if mixed with a little lobster, it will take on the taste. For that reason it is known as a flavour carrier and can be combined with more expensive seafoods to reduce costs. Bizarre-looking, it is often described as a large rounded head connected to a tail. The only edible portion of the fish is the tail, which is suitable for almost any method of cooking. It is quickly gaining popularity because of its low fat content.

Ocean Catfish — lean

Ocean Perch — lean: a.k.a. redfish, rosefish or sea perch. Firm, white, fine-textured flesh. Very versatile, with a mild flavour. Usually 6 fillets per 1 lb/500 g; allow 2 per person.

Orange Roughy — lean

Perch — lean: white-fleshed small fish. Good pan dressed or cooked as fillets.

Pike — lean: flesh is a beautiful white colour when cooked. Be sure to remove all bones.

Pollock (Alaskan or Atlantic) — lean: a.k.a. Boston Bluefish. The finest feature of this fish is the fact that it is bone free. Snow-white flesh is delicate and firm. Alaskan pollock is more delicate in flavour than North Atlantic pollock, which can have a grey tinge to the flesh.

Pompano — fat: delicious but often expensive.

Porgy — lean: small fish; good for pan-frying.

Red Snapper — lean: rich, sweet taste, juicy; firm flesh. Very versatile.

Redfish — lean: see Ocean Perch.

Rockfish — lean: flesh is firm textured and mild tasting.

Sablefish — fat: see Black Cod.

Salmon — fat: highly revered as both a wild and farmed fish. Pink to deep orange flesh, very flavourful, firm texture. Very versatile. Do not overcook — it becomes dry and tough.

Sardines — fat

Scrod — lean

Sea Bass — lean: firm white flesh. Versatile.

Shad — fat: a member of the herring family, with sweet, delicate meat. Can be very bony.

Shark — lean: comparable to Swordfish.

Shellfish — lean

Smelt — fat: small, allow 10 to 14 per person (1 lb/500 g for 2 people). Best eaten very fresh or frozen. Debone large fish only. Flavourful; usually fried.

Sole — lean: a flounder, with delicate taste and texture. Very versatile. Dover sole is only caught in European waters. Our species is known as lemon sole, blackback, winter flounder, American plaice, Atlantic halibut, sanddab, and summer flounder, depending on where it is caught and by whom.

Splake — fat: a cross between lake trout and speckled trout that is being released into lakes all through Ontario's cottage country to replace dwindling lake trout stocks. Similar to lake trout in appearance, taste and texture; has striking, almost pumpkin-orange flesh.

Squid — fat: delicate flavour. Do not overcook or it will become tough and rubbery. 1 lb/500 g serves 2 to 3 people. Best baked, stuffed or fried.

Striped Bass — fat: white, flaky flesh. Versatile.

Swordfish — fat: firm, delicious flesh. Well suited to grilling, broiling. Be careful not to overcook — should be moist, not dry.

Tilefish — lean: has white-grey flesh which is firm yet tender; similar in texture to lobster and scallops. Versatile.

Trout (Lake or Rainbow) — fat: when being purchased, should have fresh odour in the belly area. Cultivated successfully and readily available.

Trout (Sea) — lean

Tuna — fat: fresh tuna is very flavourful, with firm-textured flesh. If there is a dark midline strip of flesh, remove it — the flavour is very strong. Larger tuna — bluefin, bonita and skipjack — may need to be soaked in a light brine in the refrigerator for 1 hour, if red with blood. Not necessary with smaller albacore, blackfin or yellowfin.

Walleye — fat: flaky, white flesh. Unlike other fish, whose clear eyes indicate freshness, a milky eye is a normal characteristic of its appearance. Often called a pike, the walleye is actually a member of the perch family.

Whitefish — fat: chewy with snowy white flesh; related to salmon and trout.

Whiting — lean: see Hake.

Molluscs

Canadian mollusc producers are required by law to place tags on each box or bag of shellfish that tell when it was harvested, the name of the shipper and harvester, and the location of the harvest. The quality control of the product begins with the testing of the waters where the molluscs are grown (often more than once a week) and continues through to your table. A system of tests and checks is in place in all processing plants (for all seafood, not just molluscs). This quality control has had a great positive effect on the whole industry and has established a reputation for Canadian seafood as second to none in the world.

Oysters, mussels, clams and quahaugs are all members of the mollusc family, meaning that they are bivalves with two shells hinged at one end. Molluscs are good for you: a serving of 6 oysters, 12 mussels, or 6 to 8 clams or quahaugs will provide excellent protein, little fat, little salt and numerous vitamins and minerals. They are easily cooked and economical. It might surprise you to know that a serving of any mollusc is often less expensive than other protein alternatives. Molluscs also take less time to prepare, are always tender and are assured crowd pleasers.

Clams and Quahaugs

Although they are members of the mollusc family, clams can be a bit confusing because so many people seem to have given them different names. Eastern clams, soft-shell or steamer, are best in summer and usually enjoyed steamed or fried. Hard-shell quahaug clams, which received their name from the Algonquin Indians, are used for soups and sauces. They are called "little-necks" when small, "cherrystone" when of medium size and "chowder" when large. Quahaugs are available all year long, except mid-winter. To shuck, or open, quahaugs refer to the instructions under oysters.

Buying:

When buying clams or any other shellfish, check to see that they are alive. The shell should be tightly closed, or should close when tapped. A gaping shell that doesn't close when tapped indicates that the shellfish is no longer alive and should be discarded. If you are buying shucked clams, make sure they are plump and pale to deep orange in colour and have clear liquor. Allow 6 to 8 clams per serving.

Storing:

Store in a cool, humid place at 33-40°F/1-4°C. Do not cover — the crisper of the refrigerator is good. You can store them on ice, but *do not* put under ice or cold water. Do not store in a tightly sealed plastic bag.

Freezing:

If you bring home a good supply of clams, don't hesitate to freeze them. Remove the meat from the shells. Freeze them in their own juices, packed and tightly sealed. They will keep 4 to 6 months. Do not refreeze.

Mussels

These delicious shellfish are really coming into their own as a result of aquaculture. They can be eaten simply steamed or in numerous recipes. Generally, they can be substituted for clams or oysters in recipes.

There are several varieties of cultured or farmed mussels available year round, at a very reasonable price. They should be presented cleaned, with their "beards" (the thread-like matter that holds them in place under the water, called the "byssus") removed. Cultured mussels are sand free and generally hold full-bodied meats that are delicious.

Buying:

This can be a little confusing because wild and cultured mussels act differently. Ask which you are getting, and always opt for cultured if the choice is available. They have fuller meat, no sand or grit, and are cleaner and easier to handle. To tell the difference yourself, look at the shells. Cultured or cultivated mussels have shiny blackish-blue shells, free of blemish from other sea creatures, and are usually larger and more consistent in size. Wild mussels are usually a duller bluish colour with white erosion marks, and often have seaweed and barnacles attached, or marks that indicate where these were attached. They may have black threads near the hinge called byssus threads — the mussel uses these to anchor itself. They should be removed before eating. Cut them off with scissors or pull them out with a quick tug.

Cultured mussels are most frequently marketed live in the shell. It used to be said that mussels must be closed to be good. That is true of wild ones, but is not so with the cultured type. They often open quite wide when undisturbed. Check the open shells by tapping them. If they do not close when firmly tapped, they should be discarded. Byssus threads are usually removed from cultured mussels.

Your nose will tell you if the product is fresh. If there is any unpleasant odour, do NOT buy it. Your eyes will also pick out old, dried shells.

As for quantity — as a rule, allow 12 mussels per serving.

Storing:

Mussels are best stored in the bag in which they were shipped. Generally the bags are mesh, allowing air to circulate around them. Often you cannot have access to the shipping bag, but the container used to store mussels should have proper drainage to prevent those at the bottom from drowning. As well, it should not be too deep, as the mussels near the bottom may smother. I save the mesh bags onions come in for the purpose of storing mussels. *Never* store them in a closed plastic bag. Cover them with a damp cloth or wet newspaper and store in the coolest part of your refrigerator. The ideal storage temperature is 33-40°F/1-4°C. Use within 5 days.

Cooking:

Steaming — Any aficionado will tell you that all you need to do to cook mussels is to pop them into a pot, put a lid on and cook them for sufficient time for the shells to open. The theory is that there is enough juice in the mussel for steaming, and that added water or liquid is unnecessary. This is perfectly true for healthy, well-looked-after mussels. However, the addition of a few goodies to your cooking pot will produce a wonderful broth which Europeans, in particular, love to sop up with bread.

The following steaming method is a favourite in Belgium. It is a little heavy in butter for today's tastes, but there is no doubt that the broth is wonderful!

4 lbs	mussels, cleaned	2 kg
1 cup	celery leaves, chopped	250 mL
½ cup	butter	125 mL
½ cup	parsley, minced	125 mL
¼ cup	chives, snipped	60 mL
1 cup	dry white wine	250 mL
¼ cup	lemon juice	60 mL

In heavy stainless steel or enamelled saucepan, sauté celery leaves in butter over medium-high heat for 3 minutes, or until softened. Add parsley and chives and sauté 1 minute. Add mussels, wine and lemon juice. Bring to boil over high heat, turn heat down to medium-high and steam mussels, covered, 5 to 6 minutes or until shells have opened. Discard any unopened mussels.

If you plan to eat mussels hot, put into heated bowl or simply drain off broth and take to table in cooking pot. Broth should be strained through coffee filter and placed on table for those who wish to use it for dipping bread or mussel meats.

Serves 4, or use mussel meats in salad or other dish.

Note: If you have broth left over, strain and freeze it in ice cube trays to use when a recipe calls for clam juice or fish stock.

Microwaving — Just place mussels on a shallow microwave-safe dish, add ¼ cup/60 mL hot water and cook at high temperature for 4 to 5 minutes.

Roasting in the Oven — Place mussels in an iron frypan or in a shallow pan in a hot oven until shells open fully. A small amount of liquid can be used, if necessary.

Barbecuing — Lay mussels flat on the grill 4 or 5 inches/10 or 12 cm above the hot coal. Cover with a sheet of aluminum foil. Cook the mussels until their shells open and meats become loose from the shells (about 5 minutes). Be careful when removing mussels from the grill, as the bottom shell will be full of liquor, and very hot. Try not to spill the liquor — it is very good.

Serving:

Steamed mussels and clams are often served in the shell with dipping butter or sauce on the side. You can use a fork to remove the meat, or use the shell of another mussel or your fingers. Above all — enjoy!

Oysters

Oysters may be eaten in a variety of ways (stews, soups, sandwiches, souffles, fried, baked and so on). True aficionados will tell you that oysters should be eaten on the half-shell, served with a squeeze of lemon and a drop of Tabasco or cocktail sauce, according to locale and taste. They are an excellent source of nutrients, proteins and minerals, and are low in fat content. The P.E.I. Department of Fisheries says that an average serving of six Malpeque oysters will supply more than a daily allowance of copper and iron. They add: "There are not too many foods better balanced nutritionally than oysters."

Many different oysters are readily available today. We are most familiar with the Malpeque, which is harvested in Prince Edward Island from deep beds and shipped around the world. Our Malpeques are noted for their "keeping quality" as well as their flavour, taste and appearance. Under ideal conditions, they have been known to keep for three months, and in past years Islanders have kept Malpeque Oysters from freeze-up until early spring with no spoilage problems.

Our local oysters, along with many other varieties, are successfully cultivated. Seed oysters are produced for leaseholders who use oyster shells and wooden veneer rings to collect young oysters during spatfall (spawning). These young oysters are then utilized in the development of managed oyster areas or leaseholds.

Buying:

Oysters can be purchased live in the shell, shucked fresh, shucked and frozen, and canned. When purchasing fresh, live oysters, make certain the shells are tightly closed. A gaping shell indicates a dead oyster, which is inedible. As a rule, allow six medium-large oysters per serving.

Storing:

Do not freeze oysters in the shell. You can freeze shucked oysters successfully. However, they must be kept frozen until ready to eat. Do not refreeze. The proper temperature for storing oysters is 35-40°F/2-4°C, in as humid a temperature as possible — a good place is the crisper of your refrigerator.

Do not cover oysters and do not store them in a sealed plastic bag. Do not put them under ice or water, although they can be stored on top of ice. Care should be taken to avoid damaging the shell. Bottom mud may adhere to the shell, although they are usually sufficiently clean that washing prior to storage is unnecessary. Occasionally you may find a worm on the outside of the shell, usually if there is mud present. These are not oyster worms and in no way affect the oyster in the shell. They are natural residents of the environment where oysters live — the bottom of the sea in coastal areas.

Freezing:

To freeze oysters, remove meat from the shells before freezing. Place individual oysters in ice cube trays and cover them with oyster juice or weak brine. When frozen, pop out the cubes and store them in freezer bags. This way, you can thaw out as many as needed. Oysters keep for 4 to 6 months. Do not refreeze.

Serving on the Half-Shell:

Wash oysters under cool running water and, if necessary, scrub with a brush. Do not allow oysters to stand in water. Shells are best opened with a short, sharp, thick oyster knife. A heavy leather glove will protect your hand from the sharp shell. Hold the oyster with the deep half of the shell down. Insert the knife between the shells near the hinge. Work in the knife, and run it around the edge of the shell to cut the muscle. With a twisting motion, pry the shells apart. Sever the muscle (in the top shell) holding the shells together. Separate the shells, discarding the top, and sever the bottom muscle. Retain as much juice as possible and serve the oyster in it. An oyster knife is designed with a wedge-shaped blade to withstand the pressure required to open oysters — it's a good investment.

Scallops

Scallops seem to come in all sizes. Part of the variance is attributable to the type of scallop, where it is fished and its age. If you get big ones, try to find ones uniform in size so that they will all cook together. Large ones can also be cut in half or quartered to "stretch" them and make cooking easier. Remember to never overcook. Scallops are delicate, tender and very tasty. Overcooking can turn them into flavourless, chewy lumps.

Buying:

Look for smooth, plump meats that are slippery-looking but not slimy. Scallops packed in containers should be almost free of liquid and have a fresh odour. A trick disreputable retailers use is to add water to fresh scallops to bulk them up. The meat quickly looses its flavour and quality — it can lose its pink tinge and edges can become white and dried looking. Allow 2 lb/1 kg of scallops for 6 people.

Storing:

Scallops are best used the same day, but may be held for up to 2 days if the container is iced. Frozen scallops should be stored at the freezing point or below and can be held for 3 to 4 months. Once frozen, scallops can be used in any recipe except those calling for raw scallops.

Freezing:

Use the freshest scallops available. Pack them tightly in freezer containers and cover with a little brine (1 tbsp/15 mL salt to 1 cup/250 mL water), leaving ½ inch/1.25 cm of head space for expansion. I also have a lot of success putting them in heavy duty freezer bags, squeezing out all air and tightly sealing. This is my preferred method because all you have is scallops and their natural juices.

Cooking:

Scallops require minimal cooking — about 5 minutes to poach, 6 to sauté or 10 to broil, at the most! Overcooking is the most common mistake people make with scallops. If sautéeing or frying, make sure that the scallops are dry and the pan is hot, to prevent burning and sticking.

Crustaceans

Crab

Buying:

Crab meat, cooked and removed from the shell, is readily available in several forms: canned, frozen or fresh. Legs and whole crab are also available, fresh or frozen. Freshly packed crab meat should be kept in the refrigerator and used by the recommended date (no more than 3 days after purchase). Frozen products can be kept in your freezer for several months. Make sure they are in good condition when you purchase them, with no freezer burn or heavy frost build up. Crab meat terminology, to keep in mind when buying:

Lump or Backfin: Solid pieces, or lumps, of delicious white meat taken from the body muscles of the crab. Some folks say this is the best part, particularly as it contains little shell or cartilage. Lump or backfin works well in salads or dishes where you want definite chunks of meat.

Regular: These small pieces of savory white meat are usually from the body and are great for sandwiches, crab cakes, dips, salads and even casseroles — anywhere meat can be flaked or small pieces are needed. The flavour is excellent, and it usually costs less, but it will have to be carefully picked over for pieces of shell or cartilage.

Claws or Legs: This meat is often sold in the shell and is good for seafood boils, stews or other such dishes. Depending on the type of crab, the meat removed from the claw has a brownish tint and will be quite thin. It is best used in sandwiches or soups.

Special Mix: Usually contains a mix of lump and regular meat.

Live crabs should be packed in seaweed or damp paper. They can be stored directly in their shipping containers until ready to prepare. Do not allow fresh water to come in direct contact with crabs — it will kill them.

Lobster

Buying:

Consumers now have an option that has been the secret of many fine restaurants for years — the option of purchasing lobster fresh or frozen. Learn to select according to the end use and you will enjoy the same ease of preparation and cost effectiveness that chefs enjoy.

Seafood outlets often remove and freeze the meat from lobster they have cooked ahead. Freezing allows them to maintain the flavour and hold the product. Or, you can purchase frozen meat in the grocery store in cans or vacuum packs. Ask your retailer about both products if they are not readily visible.

Frozen lobster meat can be used by inventive cooks to enhance a multitude of delightful presentations. Each 11.3 oz/320 g can, for example, contains the meat of four to six small lobsters. As it is pre-cooked and removed from the shell, there is no shrinkage or loss, making it good value for the money. To thaw, place the unopened can or vacuum pack in cold water for approximately 2 hours. Time needed for thawing will vary according to the size of your package. Drain well before using. Once thawed, refrigerate the meat until ready to use. Then separate the meat and try the following uses:

- Body, leg and broken meat pieces are excellent in salads, sandwiches, chowders, bisques or stews — anywhere you might use chopped meat.

- Claw meat is tender and succulent, ideal for garnishing or in appetizers as well as in dishes where it will be a focal point.

- Tails can be sliced into medallions for a very attractive presentation in appetizers, salads or main dishes. They are also very good when left whole to float in a bouillabaisse, or stew.

- Tails and claws are wonderful skewered for the grill or tempura.

Storing:

Live lobster should be packed in seaweed or damp paper. They can be stored directly in their shipping containers until ready to prepare. As with crab, do not allow fresh water to come in direct contact with lobster — it will kill them.

Freezing:

When freezing lobster meat, freeze some cut-up chunks in whole milk and include the thawed liquid along with the meat in cooked chowders or casseroles and sauces. The milk protects the meat from freezer burn. Freezing toughens the texture only slightly.

Cooking:

Traditionally, lobster is served freshly cooked in the shell. Look for active lobster when you buy them live. The tail should curl back if pulled straight.

To cook, bring to a boil enough salted water (2 tbsp/30 mL salt per 1 qt/1 L water) to completely cover all lobster. (To quiet an active lobster, hold it under warm tap water for 1 minute — this will make the lobster sleepy and less active.) Hold each lobster by its back and plunge it headfirst into boiling water. Cover the pot and return the water to a boil. Lower the heat to bubbling, then simmer and cook the lobster 12 to 20 minutes, depending on size. Lobster are done when an antenna easily comes free.

Using Lobster Shells: When using whole lobster, the shells can serve double duty. After the meat is extracted, shells can be simmered to make a stock for use in sauces, chowders or a bisque.

Making Seafood Stock: Combine 3 well-crushed lobster shells and shells from 3 lb/1.5 kg shrimp with half a bottle of dry white wine. (Freeze shells until you have enough.) Reduce, by simmering over low heat until ½ to ⅓ of the original amount remains. Drain, strain and discard shell. The result will be a bright red sauce which can be cooled, then added to a hollandaise, velouté sauce, etc.

Making Lobster Butter: Shells can also be used to make a delicately pink, deliciously flavoured butter to use for finishing cream sauces or to serve with fish or lobster.

Dry the shell from 1 large lobster in an oven at low heat (250°F/120°C) for 15 minutes. Finely grind or pound the shell. Melt ¼ cup/60 mL butter in the top of a double boiler. Add the ground shell and 2 tbsp/30 mL water. Simmer 10 minutes, being careful not to let the liquid boil. Line a sieve with cheese cloth or fine muslin and strain the butter into a bowl of ice water. Refrigerate, and skim off butter when it hardens.

Boiling Lobster Tails: Many lobster dishes start with precooked meat, whole lobsters or tails. Our Fiery Lobster Fiesta, for example, is very attractive, and delicious, when made with lobster tails. If you have fresh lobster tails taken from the waters of the North Atlantic, they are excellent boiled up just as they are. Some imported lobster tails are from southern waters and have been frozen, and to those of us who are addicted to cold water lobster they seem to lack flavour. They benefit from being cooked in the following manner:

1 tbsp	salt	15 mL
1 tsp	cayenne pepper	5 mL
10	whole cloves	10
½	lemon	½
1	small onion, sliced	1
1 tsp	peppercorns	5 mL
4	(8 oz/250 g) lobster tails (if frozen, thaw)	4

Put salt, cayenne pepper, cloves, lemon, onion and peppercorns in large pot of water and bring to boil. Drop in lobster tails. Keep at full rolling boil for 20 minutes. Remove and use in recipe, or enjoy as is.

Serving:

Eating a whole lobster can seem a formidable task for the uninitiated. Approach it correctly, however, and it's a piece of cake. This ultimate finger food should be held by the body, using the other hand to twist the claw and knuckle from the body, then break each segment apart. Crack the claw and knuckles with a nutcracker or heavy knife on a cutting board and remove the meat with a fork, spoon (handle end) or small pick. Twist the tail to remove it from the body. Break off the flippers and push out the large piece of tail meat. Pull up the top piece of meat and it will peel back to reveal a dark vein in the centre of the tail flesh. Remove it before eating.

The shell covering the body can be removed by grasping the body itself and prying the shell away. Inside, you'll find additional white meat, the tomally and sometimes the caviar or eggs. For a final morsel, break off the small legs and nibble or squeeze out the meat — don't forget the flippers.

Shrimp

One thing you can be sure of finding in the supermarket these days is shrimp. They are available in a variety of sizes and presentations, most often frozen, and are often a bulk purchase. Bulk is an excellent way of buying, since you can handpick exactly the number you require. As shrimp become more popular, wild shrimp are harder to find. Not only are most areas being fished to capacity, shrimp are also one of the most successful farmed seafoods in the world. If you think this is something new, think again … the water farming of shrimp started in China 3,000 years ago. Today, the Chinese are among the leaders in farmed shrimp production. Thailand is also a major producer. That country, which used to be known for rice, now grows thousands of tons of shrimp in paddies too poor for rice.

I'm of the school that thinks farm-raised shrimp are better. Boats fishing for shrimp could be out as long as five days before bringing in the catch. Even under perfect conditions, with lots of ice to keep them cool, some shrimp would be five days old before reaching the packing plant. Farmed shrimp are out of the water, cleaned and packed within hours, then flash frozen to keep that "fresh caught" taste — normally, no additives or preservatives are added.

Buying:

Did you know that Canada and the United States are the only countries that purchase shrimp with heads removed? I guess we prefer not to have to deal with things that look at us! Experts will tell you that cooking with the head on will yield the very best flavour. Which type of shrimp you buy depends solely on your own preference.

The same rule applies to the shell: buy what your prefer to work with, shell on or shell off. Some stores offer an "easy-peel" type shrimp. Each shrimp has been split along the shell and deveined for easy preparation. Today you also have the choice of buying cooked or raw shrimp. If you are buying fresh, be sure to ask whether they have been previously frozen and what day they came in, to get an idea of how fresh they are. If shrimp have a fishy or ammonia smell, they are no longer fresh and should be discarded.

Raw, shell-on shrimp will yield about ¾ of their weight in cooked, peeled shrimp. Buy about ¼ lb/125 g raw shrimp to yield 3 oz/90 g cooked shrimp per serving.

Shrimp are often talked about as having a certain "count." This refers to the number of shrimp per 1 lb/500 g. For example: small shrimp average 51 to 60 per 1 lb/500 g, large 31 to 40, extra-large 26 to 30, jumbo 16 to 20 and extra colossal 4 to 6. The names may be different where you live, but the count is a good measure.

Storing:

Refrigerate or freeze shrimp as soon as possible after purchase and use within a day or two after thawing. Thaw raw shrimp in the refrigerator or with a brief rinse under cold running water.

Cooking:

Peeling and deveining shrimp is quite easy. Pull off the feathery legs on the underside of the shrimp. Remove the shell, leaving the tail intact. With a sharp knife, make a shallow cut down the length of the back (the upper curved part) to expose the vein. Pull out the vein, rinse the shrimp briefly and pat dry before cooking.

The dark "vein" that runs along the upper curve of the shrimp's back is actually part of its intestinal tract. It's harmless and tasteless and eating it can't hurt you. But if you don't like the way it looks, buy shrimp already deveined or remove the veins yourself.

The most important thing to remember when preparing shrimp is not to overcook them. Shrimp are cooked as soon as they turn pink and firm. Or, cut one open — if it's opaque throughout, it is cooked. Depending on the size of the shrimp, it takes 3 to 6 minutes to microwave, grill or stir-fry 1 lb/500 g.

Surimi

Surimi is the technical name for processed fish, usually Alaskan pollock, that is restructured into shellfish-like products. In the supermarket, surimi-based foods are usually called "imitations." They sell briskly in spite of this negative description. Consumers have discovered what the Japanese have known for centuries: derived fish products taste good. For many, especially those living inland, surimi-based foods mean the difference between enjoying the taste of crab meat in a salad or sandwich or doing without. It is generally less expensive, and more readily available, than real crab.

Surimi is not limited to crab flavoured fish, but that is the most popular use for it. Processors have also produced scallop and lobster imitators. The products are perfectly acceptable as long as they are being sold as what they are — fish which is processed and has flavourings and colouring added. Unfortunately, some restaurants sell surimi as being the real shellfish, and consumers rightfully feel ripped off.

While surimi products differ from producer to producer, it should be noted that they are generally high in sodium compared to the real thing, although the sodium content is not high compared to processed meats or even most commercially prepared soups. Surimi products also loose much of their nutritional value in the processing. Proteins, vitamins and minerals are literally washed away. Some people also question the additives used such as tripolyphosphates, sugar, sorbitol and msg. On the positive side, surimi is generally very low in fat and cholesterol. My approach to surimi is like many other things in life: be aware of what you are buying and enjoy it in moderation.

Garnishes

In this book you will often find an ingredient listed as a garnish. Usually these sprinklings of herbs, vegetable shapes and other ingredients are not absolutely necessary, but they take little time to prepare and add to both the appearance and taste of many dishes.

Seafood garnishes are wonderful when entertaining. They dress up a party platter of veggies, meats or salads, and enhance everyone's enjoyment and appreciation of what you serve. Here's a simple trick for a garnish:

Place a cherry tomato stem-side down and cut into it about ¾ of the way so that you have 6 sections, joined at the bottom. Scoop out a little pulp and seeds and fan out the tomato so that it looks like a flower. Stuff with a little crab mixed with spicy mayo or a smoked oyster (canned) and sprinkle with parsley. Use several such garnishes on party platters.

Complementary Condiments

While many of the recipes in this book include recipes for salsas, sauces, and other condiments, you should take advantage of those readily available. A wide variety of international condiments can be had at far less expense, and time, than it would take to make your own.

Salsas and chutneys prepared with fruit (such as papaya, pineapple, kiwi fruit, raspberry or mango) complement grilled fish. For example, blackened catfish is superb with papaya salsa. Tandoori-grilled tuna goes well with rhubarb chutney. Herb-flavoured mayonnaises and aioli sauces enhance grilled scallops, shrimp or lobster. Cilantro-grilled scallops with basil aioli explode with flavour. Take time to check out specialty stores and markets — you'll be sure to find some commercial preparations that suit your taste.

Superb Beginnings

Appetizers &
Side Dishes

*Here are perfect recipes for the beginning of a
white tablecloth sit-down dinner, for complementing a soup
or salad as a side dish, or for passing around as an hors
d'oeuvre. These appetizers are a combination of the artistic
and elegant, the luxurious and the creative. Some of the
more expensive seafoods are featured in this chapter —
with these recipes you can make small servings
and get away with it!*

Puffs of Prawn

This recipe makes good party fare, and it's an excellent way to use those electric deep-fryers that are now on the market. You may find it economical to buy twelve large shrimp or prawns with the shell on, and the remainder of the recommended weight in smaller, shelled shrimp. Snow crab cocktail claws, with the shell partially removed so that you can get at the meat, also work well in this recipe. Serve with a dipping sauce.

2 lb	prawns or large shrimp, uncooked, shell on	1 kg
2	green onions, minced	2
⅓ cup	bamboo shoots, minced	80 mL
1 tbsp	cornstarch	15 mL
1 tbsp	cooking or dry sherry	15 mL
2 tsp	ginger root, peeled and minced *or* ½ tsp/2 mL ground ginger	10 mL
¼ tsp	salt	1 mL
1	egg	1
3	slices white bread	3
	Vegetable oil, for frying	

Shell 12 shrimp, leaving last segment and tail intact. Butterfly each shrimp, carefully cutting partially through, lengthwise. Remove black vein along back and rinse. Pat dry with paper towels. Place on plate, opened, or cover and refrigerate.

Shell, devein and mince remaining shrimp so that they resemble ground meat. To this mixture, add onions, bamboo shoots, cornstarch, sherry, ginger, salt and egg.

Divide minced shrimp mixture into 12 equal portions. Using fingers, coat each butterflied shrimp with mixture, leaving tail bare to act as handle. Lay out piece of wax paper and tear bread into small pieces onto it. Roll shrimp in bread pieces and place on platter or cookie sheet.

Heat oil to about 325°F/160°C. Draw up basket and carefully lay shrimp in bottom so that they are not touching. Lower into hot oil and cook until golden, about 6 minutes, turning occasionally. Remove with slotted spoon and place on paper towels. Keep warm while you cook the rest.

Serves 4 as a main dish, 6 as an appetizer.

Hans' Pastry Triangles

Hans Anderegg, chef and instructor at the Culinary Institute of Canada, does cooking demonstrations as far away as Europe and Japan, usually featuring the use of seafood from Prince Edward Island. This recipe is so simple that he made it on television during a cooking segment on the local "after news" show. It's delicious too. Filo, or phyllo, pastry is available in the frozen food department of most grocery stores.

1 tbsp	butter	15 mL
1 tbsp	flour	15 mL
2	green onions, thinly sliced	2
½ cup	cream	125 mL
½ cup	lobster, chopped	125 mL
½ cup	shrimp, chopped	125 mL
¼ cup	dry white wine	60 mL
1	pkg filo pastry, thawed	1
	Butter, melted	

Melt butter in shallow saucepan; stir in flour to make roux. Stir in green onions; add cream and stir over medium-high heat until sauce thickens. Add lobster, shrimp and wine. Cook until well blended, stirring constantly. Remove from heat.

Carefully remove 1 sheet of filo from package and lay on baking sheet. Brush with melted butter. Lay another sheet of filo on top; brush with butter. Cut into 8 squares, each about the size of an envelope. Place 1 spoonful of filling on lower third. Fold bottom left corner up to form point at top right. Pick up point and fold up at centre, then fold once more to make triangle with several layers of pastry on each side.

You can now freeze or refrigerate, wrapped well, until ready to use. Before serving, brush a little melted butter over top and bake 8 to 10 minutes at 400°F/200°C.

Serves 4 to 8 (makes 8 triangles).

Fiery Lobster Fiesta

This versatile recipe can be made in several ways. The least costly and easiest is to begin with a can of frozen lobster meat which is thawed and drained well, then prepare the food in scallop shells or small individual ovenproof dishes. The more fancy method is to buy whole lobster or lobster tails, cook them in boiling water, split them in half and remove the meat, saving the shells. The meat is prepared as below, then stuffed back into the shells and baked. If you use the fancy method, plan on 4 small lobster or 4 tails (8 oz/225 g) and serve half of each as an appetizer. This recipe is also a good main course.

1	can (11.3 oz/320 g) frozen lobster meat, thawed and well drained	1
	or 1½ cups/375 mL lobster meat	
	or 4 8-oz/125-g lobster tails or small lobster	
½ cup	celery, chopped	125 mL
½ cup	onion, chopped	125 mL
½ cup	green or yellow bell pepper, chopped	125 mL
¼ cup	fresh parsley, chopped	60 mL
4 tbsp	butter	60 mL
2	hard-cooked eggs, shelled and chopped	2
1	raw egg	1
6	drops Tabasco sauce	6
2 cups	breadcrumbs, buttered	500 mL
	Salt and freshly ground black pepper, to taste	
	Milk	
	Spicy Butter (recipe follows)	

Preheat oven to 350°F/180°C. Prepare 6 scallop shells, small ovenproof dishes or lobster shells. If using lobster shells, split, then remove ribs from underside of tail shell with kitchen shears. Large pieces of lobster meat should be cut into chunks. If using canned meat, measure out about 1½ cups/375 mL and use rest in sandwiches or salads.

Sauté celery, onion, bell pepper and parsley in butter until onion is transparent. Gently mix together sautéed vegetables, lobster meat, hard-cooked eggs, raw egg, Tabasco sauce, 1 cup/250 mL breadcrumbs, salt and pepper to taste, and just enough milk to make mixture hold together.

Pile mixture high in each of 6 shells or dishes, and top with rest of breadcrumbs. Bake until brown, about 20 minutes. Serve at once with individual portion of Spicy Butter.

Serves 6 as an appetizer, 3 as a main course.

Spicy Butter:

½ lb	butter	250 g
8-10	drops Tabasco sauce	8-10

Slowly melt butter in heavy-bottomed pan over low heat. When butter is melted, stir in Tabasco sauce. Serve in individual demitasse or dipping cups.

Makes approximately 1 cup/250 mL.

Hot Crab in Avocado Shells

1	large avocado, halved, pit removed and shells reserved	1
1	lemon, juice of	1
8 oz	crab meat	250 g
5 oz	cream cheese	155 g
1 tbsp	tomato paste	15 mL
2	drops Tabasco sauce	2
2	strips smoked bacon	2

Remove flesh from avocado and mash with lemon juice. Add remaining ingredients, except bacon; mix well.

Divide and fill 2 avocado shells loosely — filling should be nicely rounded. Wrap each with strip of bacon.

Bake in preheated 375°F/190°C oven for 10 minutes, until bacon is crisp and crab mixture is warmed throughout.

Serves 2.

Potted Smoked Salmon

This recipe works equally well for any smoked fish, including trout and salmon.

8 oz	cream cheese, at room temperature	250 g
2 oz	smoked salmon	60 g
2-3 tbsp	whipping cream	30-45 mL
	White pepper, to taste	
	Dill (dried or fresh), to taste	
4-5	drops lemon juice	4-5

Combine mousse ingredients in bowl of food processor and blend until mixture is smooth. Chill at least 30 minutes. Serve with assortment of fine crackers.

Makes 1¼ cups/300 mL.

Hearts of Lobster

Although medallions made by slicing across lobster tails are sometimes used, this recipe is ideal for any precooked lobster meat. Make the tomato sauce ahead of time. The cucumber and lobster meat can also be prepared ahead, and placed in the refrigerator covered with a damp paper towel to keep them moist but not wet. This recipe makes eight individual serving plates or a lovely platter.

2-4 oz	cooked lobster meat per person (if using frozen meat, immerse package in cold water to thaw, open and drain well)	60-125 g
1	English cucumber, thinly sliced (score sides or peel, if desired)	1
	Fish roe or fresh herb sprigs, such as dill or coriander leaf, for garnish	
	Tomato Saffron Sauce (recipe follows)	

Prepare Tomato Saffron Sauce. For visual appeal, serve on pure white or black plates. Coat each plate with equal portion of Tomato Saffron Sauce. Place lobster medallions or meat pieces in heart shapes and tuck cucumber slices around each, either on individual dishes or spaced out on platter. Top with fish roe or sprig of dill, as garnish.

Serves 8.

Tomato Saffron Sauce:

1 tbsp	butter	15 mL
2	shallots, finely chopped	2
2 tsp	fresh tarragon, chopped or ½ tsp/2 mL dried tarragon, crumbled	10 mL
⅛ tsp	ground white pepper	0.5 mL
¾ cup	fish stock or bottled clam juice	180 mL
Pinch	powdered saffron	Pinch
¾ cup	Chardonnay or other dry white wine	180 mL
1½ tbsp	tomato paste	20 mL
1 cup	mayonnaise	250 mL
¾ tsp	fresh lemon juice	3 mL
	Salt and freshly ground black pepper, to taste	
Dash	Tabasco sauce	Dash

In skillet, sauté shallots in butter over medium heat for 5 to 7 minutes. Add tarragon, white pepper, fish stock, saffron and wine. Boil to reduce to about ½ cup/125 mL. Stir in tomato paste, mixing well; strain through sieve into mixing bowl and stir in mayonnaise, lemon juice, salt, black pepper and Tabasco. Set aside.

Zesty Mussels

These are especially nice if you have plates that are indented to hold five or six mussels. If you don't have such plates, experiment with ways to hold the mussel shells in place, such as setting the shells on a plate in a layer of rock salt or shredded lettuce.

1 lb	fresh mussels	500 g
2 tbsp	sour cream	30 mL
2 tbsp	mayonnaise	30 mL
1 tbsp	dry white wine	15 mL
1 tsp	Dijon mustard	5 mL
1 tsp	cilantro, chives or other herb, finely chopped	5 mL

Steam mussels 3 to 5 minutes, or until open. Remove half of each shell and loosen mussel meat. Cool mussels. Mix remaining ingredients. Spoon ½ tsp/2 mL sauce over each mussel and place on plates to serve.

Makes 6 to 8 appetizers.

Vietnamese Spring Rolls

The trick to these delicious spring rolls is to learn how to fold and roll them. You might want to practise with quarter rounds of paper first.

8	sheets rice paper, cut in quarters	8
	Caramel syrup (or beer), for moistening	
1 tsp	cornstarch dissolved in 1 tbsp/15 mL water	5 mL
	Vegetable oil, for deep-frying	
	Filling (recipe follows)	

Prepare filling. Soften rice paper by moistening in a little caramel or beer (this makes spring rolls turn nicely golden when deep fried).

Overlap 2 quarter rounds of rice paper in fan shape, by placing first round so that it reflects 6 to 9 on clock face. Place second round over first, with point in centre and curved side at top. With cornstarch dissolved in water, moisten along arch of top quarter round, about ½ inch/1 cm from edge. Place filling where point of upper fan lies on lower. Roll, by first folding over long side, then folding short side, then rolling up.

Heat oil in wok to 360°F/180°C; deep-fry spring rolls until golden. Cut into halves or thirds and serve hot with dip of soy sauce and mustard, or "nam pla" fish sauce (available in specialty stores) and vinegar.

Makes 16 rolls or 4 appetizers.

Filling:

1 oz	pork, shrimp and crab meat, minced	30 g
1 oz	dried cellophane noodles, soaked in cold water and finely chopped	30 g
2	shallots, finely chopped	2
1	clove garlic, finely chopped	1
¼	cooking apple, cut in julienne strips	¼
¼	carrot, cut in julienne strips	¼
2	green onions, finely chopped	2
1	sprig cilantro, chopped	1
⅙	small onion, finely chopped	⅙
1	egg, beaten	1

Toss together filling ingredients and squeeze gently to get rid of excess liquid.

Lobster Puffs

These are simply terrific party fare. Also good made with crab.

½ cup	butter	125 mL
1 cup	water	250 mL
1½ cups + 4 tbsp	flour	435 mL
6	eggs	6
	Tabasco sauce and red pepper (cayenne), to taste	
½ tsp	seasoned salt	2 mL
½ tsp	garlic salt	2 mL
½ tsp	celery salt	2 mL
2 cups	Gouda cheese, shredded	500 mL
2-3	green onions, thinly sliced	2-3
2 tbsp	parsley, minced	30 mL
1 lb	lobster meat, cooked and chopped	500 g
2 cups	vegetable oil, for frying	500 mL

Melt butter. Add water and bring to boil. Add flour, stirring until mixture leaves side of pan. Remove from heat.

Add eggs, 1 at a time, beating well after each addition. Stir in remaining ingredients. Taste for seasoning.

Drop mixture by teaspoonful into hot oil. Fry 5 minutes, until golden. Drain and serve.

Serves 8 to 10.

Chilled Lox Lasagna with Herbed Cheese

This recipe came from the Wisconsin Milk Marketing Board who, naturally, suggest you use cheese products from their home state. This is not always possible! Using cheese that is available to you, prepare this recipe ahead of time for an unusual appetizer or entrée. If you don't have a terrine mould, layer the lasagna on plastic wrap, cover and wrap with foil until you are ready to serve it.

2 cups	Ricotta cheese	500 mL
1½ cups	Mascarpone cheese	375 mL
2 tbsp	lemon juice	30 mL
1 tbsp	fresh basil, minced	15 mL
1 tbsp	fresh chives, chopped	15 mL
1 tbsp	fresh dill, minced	15 mL
1 tbsp	fresh tarragon, minced	15 mL
¼ tsp	white pepper	1 mL
8	(2 inch/5 cm wide) lasagna noodles, cooked and drained	8
1 lb	lox*	500 g
4 oz	caviar (whitefish is recommended), gently rinsed	125 g

Place cheeses, lemon juice, herbs and pepper in food processor container; process with steel blade until blended.

Line terrine mould with plastic wrap, allowing wrap to come over sides of pan. Layer 1 noodle, ½ cup/125 mL cheese mixture, 2 oz/60 g lox and 2 rounded tsp/10 mL caviar in pan. Repeat layers with remaining ingredients, ending with noodles. Cover and chill for several hours.

Garnish with fresh herb sprigs, and strips of lox rolled to look like a rose. Slice with warm knife.

Makes 24 appetizer servings or 8 entrée servings.

* Note: Lox is a brine-cured cold-smoked salmon. It is often saltier than other smoked salmon, although some lox has sugar added to the brine, making it taste less salty. Lox is a favourite in North America, where it is traditionally served with bagels and cream cheese. Substitute your favourite smoked salmon in this recipe, if you prefer.

Smoked Mackerel & Trout Platter
with Dilly Sauces

There are many types of wonderful smoked seafood available today, and they vary widely depending upon where you live. Here in P.E.I. we have delicious trout, mackerel, salmon, mussels and scallops, with smoked lobster coming soon. Some canned smoked seafoods, such as oysters, are always excellent fare. Check out the Grilling section of this book for an unusual recipe on smoking splake.

2 lb	assorted smoked fish and shellfish, such as mackerel, trout, oysters or mussels	1 kg
2	lemons, cut into wedges, for garnish	2
1	loaf black bread, thinly sliced, *or* crispbreads and crackers	1
	Fresh dillweed, for garnish	
	Mustard Dill Sauce (recipe follows)	
	Dill Cucumber Sauce (recipe follows)	

Cut fish into bite-size pieces; drain shellfish, if necessary. Arrange on large platter and garnish. Place black bread in basket at the side, along with 2 bowls of sauce.

Serves 4 as a meal, 8 as hors d'oeuvre or snack.

Mustard Dill Sauce:

¾ cup	mayonnaise	180 mL
⅔ cup	vegetable oil	160 mL
¼ cup	red wine vinegar, plus additional quantity to taste	60 mL
3-4 tbsp	grainy Dijon mustard	45-60 mL
2 tbsp	brown sugar	30 mL
⅔ cup	fresh dill, chopped	160 mL
	Salt and freshly ground pepper, to taste	

Whisk together all ingredients in mixing bowl, until well blended. Refrigerate at least 1 hour before serving.

Makes 2 cups/500 mL.

Dill Cucumber Sauce:
This sauce is particularly delicious with smoked fish.

	Fresh dillweed, roughly chopped	
½	English cucumber, grated	½
9 oz	natural yogurt	280 g
	Lemon juice	
	Garlic, minced, to taste	

Mix dill, cucumber and yogurt together. Add lemon juice and fresh minced garlic, to taste.

Makes 1½ to 2 cups/approximately 500 mL.

Salmon & Caper Dip

Valerie Lawton of the Fisheries Council of British Columbia suggests stuffing this dip into snow peas to make a party tray. It also works well stuffed into mushrooms or cherry tomatoes, spread on crackers or used as a dip with celery and carrots.

1	can (7 ½ oz/213 g) salmon	1
⅓ cup	capers, drained	80 mL
⅓ cup	celery, finely chopped	80 mL
2 tbsp	light sour cream or mayonnaise	30 mL
1 tsp	lemon juice	5 mL
2 tbsp	fresh parsley, cilantro or dillweed, chopped	30 mL
	Tabasco sauce, to taste (optional)	

In small bowl, flake salmon, along with juices and well-mashed bones. Add capers, celery, sour cream, lemon juice and herbs. Mix well to combine ingredients evenly. Add Tabasco sauce, to taste.

Makes 1¼ cups/310 mL.

Crab Stuffed Mushrooms

Pick through fresh mushrooms to get eight large ones, if you are using these as an appetizer or snack, and four huge ones if you're using the recipe as a main course. Make the breadcrumbs by buttering two slices of bread (crusts removed) then dropping them into the blender and pulsing. Enough juice is created by the mushroom itself to provide moisture for these yummy delights.

8	large, flat mushrooms	8
8 oz	crab meat, picked over to remove all shell and cartilage	250 g
2 oz	low-fat soft cheese	60 g
½ tsp	Tabasco sauce	2 mL
1 tbsp	chives, chopped	15 mL
2 oz	soft wholewheat breadcrumbs, buttered	60 g

Wipe mushrooms clean; remove stems and chop fine. Combine chopped stems, crab, cheese, Tabasco sauce and chives. Divide between mushrooms.

Sprinkle mushrooms with breadcrumbs and place under medium grill for 10 to 15 minutes, until golden. Watch them — they're hot!

Serves 8 as appetizer, 4 as main course.

Smoked Salmon Cheesecake

The plain breadcrumbs that coat the pan in this recipe create the "barely there" crust of the cheesecake. You can bake and refrigerate this appetizer twenty-four to thirty-six hours before serving — just allow an hour to bring it back to room temperature before serving.

1½ tbsp	butter or margarine, at room temperature	20 mL
⅓ cup	dry, plain breadcrumbs	80 mL
3½	pkgs (8 oz/227 g each) cream cheese, at room temperature	3½
4	large eggs	4
¾ cup	(3 oz/90 g) Gruyere cheese, shredded	180 mL
⅓ cup	half-and-half	80 mL
3 tbsp	fresh lemon juice	45 mL
2 tbsp	fresh dillweed, chopped *or* 1 tsp/5 mL dried dillweed	30 mL
¼ tsp	salt	1 mL
½ cup	green onions, thinly sliced	125 mL
4 oz	smoked salmon, thinly sliced and coarsely chopped	125 g
	Lemon slices	

Preheat oven to 325°F/160°C. Line cookie sheet with foil. Use butter to grease bottom and sides of 8 or 9 inch/20 or 22 cm springform pan. Add breadcrumbs; tilt and rotate pan so that breadcrumbs cover bottom and sides. Refrigerate pan while preparing filling.

Process cream cheese in food processor until smooth. Add eggs, cheese, half-and-half, lemon juice, dill and salt. Pulse to mix, just until smooth. Stir in onions and smoked salmon until blended.

Pour filling into chilled pan; place pan on lined cookie sheet. Bake 1 hour and 15 minutes or until wooden toothpick inserted near centre comes out clean. The edge may puff up and crack during baking, but will go down as cheesecake cools. Cool in pan on wire rack for 30 minutes. Remove pan sides; cool completely. Cut into 12 wedges and serve with lemon slice.

Serves 12.

Smoked Salmon with Scallioned Cream Cheese

We discovered Belgian endive a few years ago and have used it ever since as an "edible holder" for hors d'oeuvres — it tastes a lot better than soggy crackers. Belgian endives are one of the only truly fresh vegetables to be harvested in the winter in Atlantic Canada, where I live, and many other cold places. For a more artistic presentation of this recipe, you can place the cheese mixture into a piping bag with a star tip — just be sure the onion is minced very fine so that it doesn't block the tip.

3 oz	softened cream cheese	90 g
½	scallion (about ½ tbsp/7 mL), finely chopped, both white and green parts	½
6 oz	smoked salmon, thinly sliced	185 g
10	Belgian endive leaves, gently separated from head	10
Squeeze	fresh lemon juice	Squeeze
	Black pepper, freshly ground	
	Lemon zest or dill sprigs, for garnish	

Mix together cream cheese and scallion. Curl piece of smoked salmon onto each endive leaf and anchor end nearest base of leaf with dollop of cream cheese. Squeeze a few drops of lemon juice over top; add a few turns of freshly ground black or white pepper. Garnish and serve.

Mixture may be held in refrigerator one day, if lightly covered with plastic wrap.

Makes 10.

Salmon & Sweet Ginger
on Cucumber Rounds

To make entertaining easy, prepare the salmon mixture a day in advance, cover and refrigerate until ready to use.

1	can (7 ½ oz/213 g) salmon	1
1	pkg (4 oz/125 g) cream cheese, at room temperature	1
¼ tsp	soy sauce	1 mL
1 tsp	stem ginger in syrup, finely chopped	5 mL
¼ tsp	ginger syrup (or to taste)	1 mL
	English cucumber rounds, unpeeled, about ¼ inch/0.5 cm thick	
1	green onion, chopped, for garnish	1

Drain salmon and place in blender or food processor with metal blade in place. Cut cream cheese into 4 pieces and add to salmon, along with soy sauce, chopped ginger and ¼ tsp/1 mL ginger syrup. Whirl, stopping often to scrape down sides of container, until mixture is evenly blended. Test for seasonings and add another measure of ginger syrup, if desired.

Spoon 1 well-rounded tsp/5 mL salmon-ginger mixture onto each cucumber slice. Garnish with green onion.

Serves 8 to 12 as an hors d'oeuvre.

Seafood Lettuce Rollups

Good things really do come in small packages. These little surprise "packages" are perfect for cocktail finger food or for serving as a dinner-party first course. They will please the health conscious in your crowd, are simple to make and look impressive. Best of all, they can be made ahead of time — simply refrigerate until you're ready to serve. Although we have made them with salmon and shrimp, you can vary the filling for a different flavour.

1	head leaf or Boston Bib lettuce	1
1	can (7 ½ oz/213 g) salmon	1
1	dried red chili pepper *or* 1 fresh hot pepper	1
½ cup	low-fat yogurt	125 mL
1 cup	shrimp (buy tiny canned shrimp, or shrimp that is frozen, cooked and shelled)	250 mL
2 cups	alfalfa sprouts	500 mL

Wash lettuce and separate leaves. Cut large lettuce leaves in half down centre vein. Flake salmon, along with juices and well-mashed bones. Split chili pepper in half lengthwise, remove seeds and vein, finely chop and mix into yogurt.

On narrow end of each lettuce piece or leaf, place 1 tbsp/15 mL salmon. Top with 2 to 3 shrimp, about 2 tbsp/30 mL alfalfa sprouts, and dollop of yogurt. Roll into cylinder shape.

Makes about 16 rolls.

Stuffed Mussels

I deally, this first course is prepared well ahead of time, as the mussels should be well chilled and served cold.

24-30	large mussels, cleaned	24-30
⅓ cup	dry white wine	80 mL
½ cup	olive oil	125 mL
⅓ cup	pine nuts	80 mL
3 cups	onions, minced	750 mL
1 cup	long grain rice	250 mL
⅓ cup	dried currants	80 mL
2 tbsp	parsley, minced	30 mL
1 tsp	salt	5 mL
¼ tsp	ground cinnamon	2 mL
¼ tsp	allspice	2 mL

Steam mussels in wine until open. Remove. Strain liquor through sieve lined with coffee filter or cheesecloth.

In skillet, heat olive oil and lightly brown pine nuts; remove and set aside. Sauté onions until lightly coloured, about 10 minutes. Stir in rice, currants, parsley, salt, cinnamon, allspice, reserved liquor and enough water to cover rice by ½ inch/1 cm. Bring liquid to boil and reduce heat; tightly cover and simmer for 20 minutes, or until rice is cooked.

While rice is cooking, shell mussels, reserving shells. Remove black rims from mussels, then stir mussels and pine nuts into rice mixture. Allow to cool.

Separate mussel shells, filling deeper half with stuffing, mounded up; top with other shell. Press down to close halves.

Arrange on platter, cover and chill until ready to serve — the mussels should be cold when served.

Serves 6.

Oysters Poached in Champagne

Have you ever watched one of those movies where people sip on fluted glasses of "bubbly" as they glide across the floor in a tightly meshed waltz, gazing into each others' eyes with star-glazed passion. Sighhhhh. If you want to set that type of romantic scene at your next dinner party, then consider these luscious oysters.

1	lemon, juice and zest of	1
32	oysters in shell, scrubbed clean and shucked, reserving liquor and deep side of shell	32
2 cups	champagne or sparkling wine	500 mL
½ tsp	parsley, chopped	2 mL
½ tsp	dry mustard	2 mL
½ tsp	chervil	2 mL
1 tbsp	whole black peppercorns	15 mL
1 cup	spinach leaves, washed	125 mL
2 tbsp	scallions, cut in julienne strips	30 mL
¼ cup	sweet red peppers, cut in julienne strips	60 mL
1 tbsp	clarified butter, or extra virgin olive oil	15 mL
	Salt and pepper, to taste	

Place lemon zest in cold water and heat or poach 1 minute to remove bitterness. Drain and reserve.

Combine oysters and their liquor, champagne, parsley, mustard, chervil and peppercorns in pan; poach 1 minute. Remove oysters and place in shells. (Have shells placed on serving plates.)

Over medium heat, reduce poaching liquid to 1 cup/250 mL and spoon over oysters. While cooking, sauté spinach, scallions, lemon zest and peppers in butter or olive oil for 1 minute. Deglaze sauté pan by pouring in lemon juice; season mixture with salt and pepper.

Divide vegetables and serve beside oysters. Spoon lemon juice over vegetables.

Serves 8.

Sea Scallops with Orange & Saffron

These make delightful appetizers when served in scallop shells decorated with orange zest or a twist of orange. René Verdon, of *Le Trignon* in San Francisco, suggests serving this dish — which he describes as the ultimate in simplicity — as a main course with fresh steamed vegetables and rice or pasta.

1 lb	fresh scallops (if large, cut into thirds)	500 g
1	orange, juice and zest of	1
1	tomato, skinned, seeded and diced	1
½ tsp	saffron threads	2 mL
	Salt and pepper, to taste	
1 tsp	butter	5 mL
1	small shallot, chopped	1
2 tbsp	dry white wine	30 mL
¼ cup	cream	60 mL
2 tbsp	parsley, chopped (optional)	30 mL
6	scallop shells (optional)	6

Place scallops in bowl; add juice and zest of orange, diced tomatoes, saffron and salt and pepper. Marinate 3 to 4 hours, or longer, in refrigerator.

Strain scallops, reserving marinade. Place butter and shallots in sauté pan over medium heat. Add scallops and sauté 1 minute, being careful not to overcook. Remove scallops and add marinade, white wine and cream. Reduce liquid by half by cooking gently and stirring often. Return scallops to pan and bring to boil; add salt and pepper to taste, if needed. Transfer to hot serving dishes or scallop shells. Sprinkle with parsley.

Serves 6 as an appetizer, 4 as a main course.

Shrimp Balls

These are nice served on a tray of "pass-around" hors d'oeuvres or as a snack. Just stick a toothpick (fancy ones for a special occasion) in each shrimp ball and let people help themselves.

1 lb	raw shrimp, shells removed	500 g
1	small onion, finely chopped	1
1	egg, beaten	1
3 tbsp	parsley, chopped	45 mL
4 tbsp	green onions, chopped	60 mL
½-1 tsp	hot pepper sauce	2-5 mL
	Salt and pepper, to taste	
	Oil, for deep-frying	

Place shrimp (make sure shell, including tail, is removed) and onion in food processor; pulse until smooth. Add remaining ingredients, except oil, and mix well.

Heat cooking oil to 350°F/180°C. Drop heaped teaspoonfuls of prawn mixture into hot oil and fry 3 to 4 minutes, until crisp and golden. Drain well on paper towels. Keep warm in oven until ready to serve.

Serves 4.

Marinated Turbot

This recipe and the one following are among those used by the Canadian Native Culinary Team during the 1992 Frankfurt Culinary Olympic competitions. They came from Bertha Sky, a team member who conducts Native cooking workshops on the Six Nations Reserve near Brantford, Ontario. She and her teammates brought home seven gold medals from that competition. Remember, once cured, these marinated fish dishes should be eaten right away.

1	lemon, juice of	1
3 oz	olive oil	90 mL
2 tsp	wild onion (or shallots), chopped	10 mL
2 oz	sea salt	60 mL
2 oz	white sugar	60 mL
1 tsp	pink, cracked peppercorns	5 mL
3 lb	turbot (fillet)	1.5 kg

Combine lemon juice, olive oil and chopped onion. Set aside. Mix sea salt, white sugar and peppercorns.

Carefully remove all bones from turbot; coat with liquid mixture. Cover with dry mixture. Wrap fish tightly in cheesecloth and place in refrigerator for 30 hours.

Remove all ingredients and slice like smoked salmon.

Makes approximately 3 lbs/1.5 kg.

Marinated Arctic Char

Slice this fish like smoked salmon and enjoy it the same way. The surplus liquid can be mixed with mayonnaise and mustard as a sauce.

3 lb	Arctic Char (fillet)	1.5 kg
3 oz	sea salt	90 mL
2 oz	brown sugar	60 mL
4 oz	wild anise or fresh dill	120 mL
2 oz	olive oil	60 mL
1 tsp	peppercorns, coarsely ground	5 mL

Remove all bones from fillets. Mix together sea salt, brown sugar, anise, olive oil and peppercorns. Cover fish with mixture and store in refrigerator. Marinate 24 hours, occasionally moistening fish with liquid it produces. Slice thinly and use as you would smoked salmon.

Makes 3 lbs/1.5 kg.

Lobster Elizabeth

This recipe comes from *Elmwood Heritage Inn* in Charlottetown, Prince Edward Island, where it was invented to tantalize the palates of guests. It was the winner in a contest at which I was a judge, and has been a favourite of mine ever since.

1	can (11.3 oz/320 g) frozen lobster meat, thawed *or* 1½ cups/375 mL cooked lobster meat	1
½	medium onion, very finely chopped	½
3 tbsp	olive oil	45 mL
3 tbsp	butter	45 mL
1	large garlic clove	1
4 tbsp	fresh parsley, chopped	60 mL
2 tsp	dill weed	10 mL
2	tomatoes, peeled and chopped	2
1½ tbsp	fresh lime juice	20 mL
1 tbsp	Pernod	15 mL
	Salt and white pepper, to taste	
	Linguini, cooked *al dente*	

Drain lobster well, then coarsely chop, leaving claw pieces intact. Cut tails crosswise into rounds.

Sauté onion in olive oil and butter until soft and just golden. Add garlic and stir. Add parsley and dill; stir. Add tomatoes add cook 5 minutes. Add lime juice and Pernod. Season sauce with salt and pepper.

When linguini is ready to serve, add lobster and sauce; toss until heated through. Do not cook too long, or lobster will toughen. Serve on hot plates garnished with lime and fresh parsley or dill.

Serves 4 as an appetizer.

Lobster Croustades

Canadian West Coast cookbook writer Kasey Wilson claims that these croustades are "fantastic," and she's right. She adds: "I never can brush the insides of the darn cups with butter; so I always butter the bread (both sides) before I push it into the muffin cups."

18	thin slices white bread, cut in 3 inch/8 cm rounds	18
2 tbsp	butter, softened	30 mL
½ lb	lobster meat, cooked, cut into small pieces	250 g
1 tbsp	red, green or yellow peppers, finely chopped	15 mL
1 tsp	lemon juice	5 mL
1½ tbsp	mayonnaise (to bind)	20 mL
4	drops Tabasco sauce	4
	Pepper, to taste	

Preheat oven to 350°F/180°C. Brush muffin tins with butter. Fit bread rounds into each mould to form cup. Brush inside with butter.

Combine lobster, peppers, lemon juice, Tabasco and pepper, with enough mayonnaise to bind. Spoon into cups and bake 10 minutes. Serve immediately.

Makes 18 croustades.

Just Peachy Appetizers

1	can (6 oz/170 g) crab meat	1
¼ cup	celery, chopped	60 mL
¼ cup	mayonnaise	60 mL
1 tbsp	green onion, minced	15 mL
1 tsp	lemon juice	5 mL
½ tsp	Worcestershire sauce	2 mL
	Salt and pepper, to taste	
1	egg white	1
5	peaches	5

Drain and flake crab meat. In small bowl, combine crab meat, celery, mayonnaise, onion, lemon juice, Worcestershire, salt and pepper. In separate bowl, beat egg white until stiff but not dry. Fold into crab mixture.

Preheat broiler. Peel, pit and quarter peaches. Make lengthwise slashes to divide each quarter into thirds. Slashes should be deep enough to allow pieces to fan out (outer 2 sections should lie flat with middle piece standing upright), but should not go completely through peaches. Place peach pieces on lightly greased cookie sheet.

Spoon crab mixture into grooves between peach sections. Broil 6 to 8 inches/15 to 20 cm from heating element for 4 to 5 minutes, or until lightly browned.

Makes 20 appetizers.

Cheesy Baked Mussels

Since most of our friends are mussel lovers, we usually allow at least eight of these per person (that is, sixteen mussels). For a party you are probably safe with four (or eight mussels) of these delicious appetizers for each person.

Mussels, steamed in ⅛ cup/30 mL white wine just until shells open (do not overcook)

Melted butter or olive oil (or combination)

Breadcrumbs

Parmesan or Swiss cheese, grated

Parsley, finely chopped

Garlic, minced

Pepper, to taste

Lemons

Once mussels have cooled, remove meats from shells and set aside, reserving broth. Break mussel shells apart, keeping largest. Fill each reserved shell with 2 mussel meats and arrange on flat, heat-proof serving platter.

Pour a little melted butter or olive oil over each shell, then sprinkle lightly with breadcrumbs mixed with equal quantity of cheese, parsley, garlic and pepper to taste. Strain a little of reserved broth over each shell, just to moisten. Heat in moderate oven until warm and serve immediately with lemon wedges.

Allow 8 to 16 mussels per person.

Quick Salmon Mousse

This light, savoury mousse does double duty as a stuffing for veggies such as cherry tomatoes, or tiny puff pastry shells, or as a dip.

1	can (7 ½ oz/213 g) salmon, drained	1
2 tbsp	light sour cream	30 mL
2 tbsp	light mayonnaise	30 mL
2 tsp	lemon juice	10 mL
¼ tsp	Worcestershire sauce	1 mL
Dash	hot pepper sauce	Dash
	Green onions or cilantro, minced	

In food processor, process salmon until smooth. Add sour cream, mayonnaise, lemon juice, Worcestershire sauce and hot pepper sauce; process for 30 seconds. Serve as dip, or spoon into mushroom caps, Belgian endive leaves or hollowed-out cherry tomatoes. Sprinkle with minced green onions or cilantro.

Makes about 1 cup/250 mL.

Finger Fun

Snacks & Party Food

Here are easy-to-prepare recipes that make wonderful party food and also make great casual foods such as pizza, kids' treats and nibblers — the kind of thing you would serve to drop-in visitors or the gang when they are gathered to watch a game on TV.

Nabemono (Asian One Pot Cooking)

N abemono is a technique whereby everyone does their own cooking, much in the style of the old fondue. The difference is that this method uses steaming stock instead of heavy cheeses or oils.

Traditionally, an earthenware casserole full of steaming stock is placed in the centre of the table on a heating unit. Platters of beautifully arranged seafood or meat, vegetables and noodles are placed within easy reach. This food will have been cut into portions easy to cook, and is usually both beautiful to look at and as fresh as can be. Each person is provided with chopsticks for cooking, and another set for eating. Spicy condiments and dipping sauces are placed around the table.

Nabemono is perfect party fare. If you have a large crowd, set up several cooking locations. The very best part of this method of cooking is the fact that the host or hostess prepares everything ahead of time and is able to sit down and participate in this incredibly social occasion. Make people use the chopsticks — the inexperience of many guests will contribute to fun all around.

Shabu Shabu (Hot Pot)

W e first experienced this wonderful dish at the *Banff Springs Hotel* in Alberta, where we sat at a bar and each had our own cooking pots, plates of seafood and vegetables, and dipping sauces. The name of the dish imitates the sound that is made as ingredients are swished around in the steaming broth.

2 lb	fresh seafood, cut into bite-size portions (a combination of salmon, white fish, shrimp, scallops)	1 kg
¼-½ lb	mushrooms, cleaned (try some exotics or use button)	125-250 g
¼-½ lb	spinach leaves, washed and trimmed	125-250 g
4	Chinese cabbage leaves, sliced crossways	4
1	cake tofu, cut into 6 to 12 pieces	1
2-4 oz	harusame (transparent rice noodles), soaked in warm water for 5 minutes	60-125 g
1	carrot, "flower cut"	1
½ lb	udon (similar to spaghetti, but softer and made from wheat or corn flour), boiled for 8 minutes	250 g
18	ginko nuts, shelled (optional)	18
6	lemon wedges	6
	Sesame Paste Sauce (recipe follows)	
	Soy with Momiji-oroshi (recipe follows)	
	Shabu-Shabu Cooking Broth (recipe follows) or water plus 4 inch/10 cm square piece of Konbu (seaweed)	

Neatly arrange seafood on large platter; garnish. On second platter, arrange vegetables and harusame. Skewer ginko nuts on toothpicks (3 on each) and add to platter. Garnish with lemon. Place udon in separate bowl. Fill hoko name (Mongolian hot pot), fondue pot or other pot ¾ full of stock mixture, or use plain water with Konbu. Bring to boil; if using Konbu, remove from pot once liquid boils.

Now the fun begins: Have everyone help themselves to ingredients from platters. Use chopsticks to swish ingredients around in broth. Vegetables take a little longer to cook, so may be dropped and retrieved. Food just out of pot should be dipped into either sauce and eaten immediately. Udon and harusame also get a brief dip in the stock pot.

If guests are having trouble with their chopsticks, make the chopsticks into "cheaters": Put an elastic band around 2 chopsticks, just ½ inch/1 cm down from top. Place small roll of paper between the two sticks, just below elastic. This will make chopsticks into pinchers, and much easier to use.

Serves 6.

Sesame Paste Sauce:

5 oz	white sesame seeds	155 g
4 fl oz	soybean milk	125 mL
3 tbsp	soy sauce	45 mL
1 cup	water	250 mL
Drop	chili oil	Drop

Blend all ingredients in blender. Serve in several small bowls.

Soy with Momiji-oroshi:

1 inch	piece daikon (white radish)	2.5 cm
1	dried hot red pepper, cut open and seeds discarded, then sliced	1
1	radish, peeled	1
4 tbsp	spring onion, minced	60 mL
	Soy sauce	

Poke several holes around middle of peeled daikon. Fit pepper into holes and grate daikon and radish into small bowl. Pepper flakes which appear in radish mounds give this condiment its name, meaning "red maple grate." Place mixture in one small bowl, and minced onion in another.

Pour 2 to 3 tbsp/30 to 45 mL soy sauce into 6 small bowls and give each person a bowl. Have each person take a little of Momiji-oroshi (radish mixture) and a little spring onion, and mix into soy sauce.

Shabu-Shabu Cooking Broth:

4 cups	chicken stock	1 L
2	green onions, chopped	2
2 tbsp	coriander, coarsely chopped	30 mL
3	slices (¼ inch/0.5 cm) fresh ginger root	3
1	clove garlic, sliced	1
1	strip (2 inches/5 cm) lemon rind	1

Place all ingredients in hot pot or fondue pot; bring to boil. Reduce heat to medium and simmer 5 minutes.

Conversation Dippers

There is something particularly enjoyable about sitting around a table with friends, dipping and dunking food into a common pot and enjoying each others' company. Cut the fruit into bite-size pieces, use pre-cooked seafood such as lobster meat, shrimp, scallops and mussels, add a bottle of sparkling white wine and you have the makings of a lovely shared time. This recipe is perfect to serve on the deck after a long hot day. When selecting the seafood, remember you must be able to pick it up on a toothpick, dunk it in the dip and get it to your mouth without it breaking.

Those who prefer a "deep-fried" flavour can use oil and seafood for a wonderful fondue. Use squid, shrimp, scallops, fatty types of fish and vegetables.

3 cups	cooked seafood, such as lobster meat*, medium shrimp, scallops or mussels	750 mL
1	honeydew melon, cut into bite-size pieces	1
2	papayas, peeled and cut into chunks	2
½	cantaloupe, cut into bite-size pieces	½
8	kiwi fruit, peeled and quartered	8
1½ cups	almonds, slivered	375 mL
	Yogurt Dip (recipes follow)**	
	Toothpicks	

* If using lobster, cut the tails into chunks and serve with claws and large pieces of meat. Reserve small pieces of meat for a salad or sandwich.

** For variety, purchase a commercially prepared fruity dressing as well.

Arrange seafood and fruit on 1 or 2 platters and place in centre of table. Place almonds, dip and toothpicks so that everyone can reach them — you may have to divide into 2 or 3 lots.

Serves 6.

Yogurt Dip #1:
Use light or low-fat ingredients, if desired.

1½ cups	plain yogurt	375 mL
1½ cups	mayonnaise	375 mL
1½ tbsp	Dijon mustard	20 mL
1 tsp	sugar, or quantity to taste	5 mL
1 tsp	poppy seeds	5 mL

Thoroughly blend together ingredients and serve in bowl suitable for dipping.

Makes 3 cups/750 mL.

Yogurt Dip # 2:
When using this dip, carry over the orange flavour by including orange slices or segments on your party platter.

1½ cups	low-fat yogurt	375 mL
1 cup	reduced-calorie mayonnaise	250 mL
½ cup	orange juice	125 mL

Whisk together ingredients in bowl until well blended. This dip also works well as salad dressing.

Makes 3 cups/750 mL.

Shrimp in Beer with Two Sauces

Try this different approach to creating a basket of shrimp.

1	bottle beer	1
1 tbsp	salt	15 mL
2 lb	jumbo shrimp, shell on	500 g
	Sweet Mustard Sauce (recipe follows)	
	Niçoise Sauce (recipe follows)	
1	lemon, cut into wedges	1

Pour beer into large saucepan, add salt and bring to boil. Add shrimp; bring back to boil and cook until all shrimp turn pink, stirring occasionally. When beer returns to boil, shrimp should be done. Drain shrimp; place on warm platter and serve with sauces and lemon.

Serves 6 to 8.

Sweet Mustard Sauce:

½ cup	prepared mustard	125 mL
2 tbsp	sugar	30 mL
2 tbsp	white vinegar	30 mL
1 tbsp	salad oil	15 mL

Mix together all ingredients until well combined.

Niçoise Sauce:

¾ cup	mayonnaise	180 mL
2 tbsp	capers, minced	30 mL
1 tbsp	anchovy paste	15 mL
1 tbsp	ketchup	15 mL
⅛ tsp	salt	0.5 mL

Combine all ingredients and mix well.

Smoked Salmon & Basil Pâté

If you are in a hurry to prepare this recipe, buy the smoked-salmon cream cheese spread at your market. It speeds things up, costs less and works wonderfully well.

½ lb	soft cream cheese	250 g
2 tbsp	fresh basil, chopped	30 mL
2 oz	smoked salmon, finely chopped	60 g
2 tbsp	red bell pepper, finely chopped	30 mL
	Almond slices (optional)	

Mix half soft cream cheese with basil. A wooden spoon or spatula works best for mixing. Mix rest of soft cream cheese with smoked salmon.

Oil pâté dish (5x2x2 inch/1 L loaf pan), or suitable dish with straight sides. Line with plastic food wrap or waxed paper, extending paper beyond edges. Work cheese and basil mixture until spreadable, then spread in bottom of prepared pan in even layer. Sprinkle red pepper over cheese, keeping ½ inch/1 cm in from edge all the way around.

Use clean spoon back or fingers to gently press red pepper into cream cheese. Smooth salmon and cheese mixture over top, being careful not to disturb peppers. It's a good idea to rap pan on counter several times, in case any air bubbles remain. Cover and chill overnight to firm up mixture.

When ready to serve, prepare serving plate. Gather extended wrap or waxed paper and gently lift out pâté. Invert onto serving plate and remove wrap. Smooth out top of pâté with spatula. Gently press almond slices into top and sides, if desired. Surround with crackers or toast rounds and serve.

Serves 6 to 8 as an hors d'oeuvre.

Seafood Enchiladas with Dijon Rancher Sauce

Because this recipe makes thirty enchiladas, it is great for a party. I think it's especially appropriate for one of those affairs where folk gather in the kitchen and help prepare the food — a great way of breaking the ice. The enchiladas are nice served with a salad containing corn niblets or baby cobs, to enhance the flavour of corn in the tortillas and keep the meal in theme.

2 tbsp	butter	30 mL
2 tbsp	flour	30 mL
2 cups	beef broth	500 mL
2 cups	tomato sauce, canned	500 mL
1	garlic clove, minced	1
¼ tsp	cayenne pepper	1 mL
¼ tsp	dried oregano	1 mL
⅛ tsp	ground cumin	0.5 mL
1 cup	Dijon mustard	250 mL
2 lb	small shrimp	500 g
2 lb	bay (small) scallops, drained	500 g
2 oz	olive oil	60 mL
30	corn tortillas	30
1¾ lb	Cheddar cheese, grated	875 g

Melt butter over medium heat; stir in flour to make roux. Cook for 5 minutes, continuing to stir so that roux does not burn. Gradually add broth until fully blended, then add tomato sauce. Simmer for 5 minutes. Add garlic, seasonings and Dijon mustard; simmer for 5 minutes. Set sauce aside.

Sauté shrimp and scallops in small batches in smoking hot oil, until just cooked. Toss with 1 cup/250 mL sauce. Divide mixture between tortillas (about ¼ cup/60 mL each) and roll loosely. Ladle about 3 oz/90 g sauce over enchiladas, sprinkle with cheese and place under broiler until cheese melts.

Serves 10 (3 each) to 15 (2 each).

Lobster Fajitas

As we entered the '90s, the traditional Mexican "skirt steak" — steak that is grilled, cut into strips and wrapped in a warm tortilla — became very popular. The enjoyment of such "finger food" has expanded to include a sometimes surprising ingredient — Canadian lobster. Fajitas with lobster blend very well into the type of social dining popular today. People are moving away from static meals where food is simply placed on a plate before them. Hands-on dining makes presentations such as a sizzling pan of soft tortillas warmed and wrapped in a cloth napkin, accompanied by an assortment of fillings and condiments, a sure winner. Taking the hot pan to the table and allowing the delicious aroma of onions, green peppers and lobster to drift throughout the room will heighten everyone's enjoyment of their meal. To serve, allow the filling to sizzle in the pan, and surround it with a variety of condiments and a basket of warm, soft tortillas.

Condiments such as melon relish, sour cream, shredded lettuce, chopped tomatoes, guacamole and black or refried beans can be served in small bowls or edible tortilla baskets. For a truly Mexican experience, consider diced pickled jalapeños, fresh cilantro, lemon wedges and chopped green onions. If your guests seem a little puzzled, it is a simple task to demonstrate rolling a fajita and encourage everyone to join in the fun.

1	can (11.3 oz/320 g) frozen lobster meat, thawed and drained *or* 1½ cups/375 mL fresh cooked lobster meat, cut into chunks	1
1	medium onion, sliced	1
	Pineapple Marinade (recipe follows)	

Marinate lobster in Pineapple Marinade for at least 2 hours, then drain. Prepare skillet in very hot oven for at least 15 minutes. Place onions in frying pan and cook very quickly. Add lobster pieces; fry 1 minute. Place all ingredients onto red-hot platter.

Serve at once, sizzling and accompanied by soft shell tortillas and condiments such as: guacamole, melon relish, sour cream, shredded lettuce and chopped tomatoes.

Serves 4 to 6.

Pineapple Marinade:

⅛ cup	cooking oil	30 mL
⅛ cup	wine vinegar	30 mL
⅛ cup	onion, finely chopped	30 mL
½ tsp	salt	2 mL
⅛ tsp	pepper	0.5 mL
½ cup	pineapple juice	125 mL

Whisk ingredients together.

Perry's Dip

It was a tradition at *Stanhope Beach Lodge* in Prince Edward Island to provide "nibblers" for guests waiting their turn at the smorgasbord or simply relaxing in the lounge area. A favourite among guests was this dip, which was often placed on a coffee table with taco chips, potato chips or corn chips. Many people asked for this recipe, which Chef Perry graciously shared with me. If you want to make it really fancy, add a few chopped chives.

1	part cream cheese	1
2	parts sour cream	2
	Garlic, minced, to taste	
	Small pieces of seafood such as crab, lobster, salmon, shrimp, clams etc. (canned pieces are fine, just drain well)	

Blend cream cheese and sour cream together. Stir in garlic. Add seafood, gently mixing well.

Shrimp Triangles

There is something about hot appetizers or snacks that never fails to create an impression. Borrow an idea from Hawaii and present guests with a platter of tempting finger foods, making one of the selections these shrimp toasts. They feature the crunchy, delicious flavour of macadamia nuts.

7 oz	cocktail shrimp (if using frozen shrimp, thaw)	215 g
⅔ cup	macadamia nuts, chopped	160 mL
1 tbsp	cornstarch	15 mL
½ tsp	sugar	2 mL
1	egg, lightly beaten	1
1 tsp	soy sauce	5 mL
½ tsp	dry sherry	2 mL
6	slices day-old, firm-textured white bread, crusts removed	6
	Vegetable oil	

Finely chop shrimp. In medium-size bowl, combine shrimp, nuts, cornstarch, sugar, egg, soy sauce and sherry. Cut each slice of bread into 4 triangles. Spread each triangle with 1 tbsp shrimp mixture; smooth top and sides with knife.

Coat skillet with ½ inch/1 cm vegetable oil and heat to 350°F/180°C. Place a few shrimp toasts into hot oil, shrimp side down; cook until golden, about 45 seconds. Turn and cook until bread is golden, about 3 seconds. Remove with slotted lifter and place on paper towels to drain.

Repeat, a few shrimp at a time, until all are cooked. Serve at once, or refrigerate and reheat when needed by placing on baking sheet, covering with foil and baking in preheated 350°F/180°C oven until hot, about 10 minutes.

Makes 24 pieces.

John's Tarragon Shrimp Dip

I had forgotten about this wonderful dip until I started going through my boxes of recipes for this book. There, I found my old cookbook from when our son was just going into his teens. He loved this recipe back then, and probably still does — I'm sending it to him in Vancouver as soon as I write this, so he can try it again. Back in the days when I made this dip, money was pretty tight. We would make it with just half a can of baby shrimp, because they were inexpensive, and I would make a sandwich out of the other half. If you want to serve this in the Edible Dip Bowl (see page 85), triple the recipe. It makes an excellent accompaniment to a raw veggie tray.

½ tsp	tarragon	2 mL
½ cup	sour cream	125 mL
8 oz	cream cheese, softened	227 g
1	can (6 ½ oz/175 mL) baby or salad shrimp, well drained	1
1½ tsp	Worcestershire sauce	7 mL
¼ tsp	salt	1 mL
½ tsp	dry mustard	2 mL
½ tsp	garlic salt	2 mL
¼ tsp	onion juice	1 mL
Dash	cayenne	Dash

Mix tarragon into sour cream and let stand 30 minutes. Beat cheese until fluffy and add sour cream. Stir in remaining ingredients. Chill and serve.

Makes approximately 2 cups/500 mL.

Hot Cheese & Crab Dip

Bring out the fondue pot and get ready to tucker into one of the most delicious — if most fattening — snacks to be found in these pages. I have a deep passion for tangy extra old Cheddar cheese, crab, and mixtures I can sit beside and dunk bread into. I just love to interact with my food, and from the way this dip disappears, I know many of my friends do as well. This recipe ages well if made ahead, but you may have to add a little wine, as it tends to thicken. Serve with chunks of crusty bread and fondue forks, or with shredded wheat wafers.

1	stick (10 oz/310 g) sharp (extra old) natural Cheddar cheese	1
1	pkg (8 oz/227 g) processed sharp cheese slices	1
¼ cup	butter	60 mL
½ cup	sauterne	125 mL
1	can (7 ½ oz/213 g) crab meat, drained	1

Cut cheeses into small pieces to make melting easier. Combine with butter and sauterne in fondue pot. Reserving a few pieces for garnish, flake or shred crab meat and add to pot. Stir over low heat and continue cooking to heat through, until cheese melts and all ingredients become smooth.

Place fondue pot in holder over heat and serve. Do not keep more than 1 day, and refrigerate if dip is not being kept hot.

Makes approximately 2 cups/500 mL.

Edible Dip Bowl

Round loaves of sourdough bread make wonderful holders for dips or salads. When using bread for dips, slice top off loaf about 1 inch/2.5 cm from top. Cut out bread from centre of loaf to form bowl, leaving ¾ inch/1.5 cm shell or bowl. Cut removed bread and top of loaf into chunks for dipping, and keep in plastic bag, to prevent drying out, until ready to serve.

When ready to serve, pour dip into "bowl" and serve with bread chunks and veggies for dunking. As dip is eaten, just break off sides of "bowl." Dip will have soaked into bread, making it absolutely delicious.

Julie's Dip

Serve this dip in an edible dip bowl, with little squares of thin dark bread or chunks of French bread for dipping. When using smoked salmon in a recipe such as this one that requires it to be chopped, ask your deli owner or seafood retailer if they have any broken slices or ends — they're less expensive.

2 cups	sour cream	500 mL
½	pkg (2½ oz/77 g) dry leek soup mix	½
¼ lb	smoked salmon, finely chopped	125 g
	Fresh dillweed, chopped	

Stir sour cream and dry soup mix together until evenly blended. Stir in salmon. Refrigerate, preferably overnight, to give soup mix a chance to soften and blend in. Garnish with chopped fresh dill.

Makes 2 cups/500 mL.

Jennifer's Mousse

A friend called one day and said she had a wonderful dish for her Christmas party, and that it was both low cal and, as she put it, "fancy enough for the queen." This is her recipe, and it's a great addition to any party or get-together, particularly because of its light fresh texture and taste. Jennifer used leftover lobster. We put in some canned crab we had on hand, and it was equally lovely.

1	envelope unflavoured gelatin	1
¼ cup	lemon juice	60 mL
½ lb	small, frozen, cooked shrimp *or* 2 cans (approximately 4 oz/120 g each) canned shrimp	250 g
1	pkg (8 oz/227 g) light cream cheese	1
1	can (7 ½ oz/213 g) quality salmon, drained skin and bone removed	1
1	can (4 ¼ oz/120 g) crab*, drained *or* equal amount of leftover lobster* or crab*	1
2	green onions, thinly sliced	2
¼ cup	red or yellow bell pepper, finely chopped	60 mL
¼ cup	fresh dill, chopped	60 mL
2 tbsp	ketchup	30 mL
Pinch	cayenne	Pinch
1¼ cups	light sour cream	310 mL
	Salt and pepper, to taste	
	Dill, green onions, or shapes cut from bell pepper, for garnish	
	Crackers, cucumber slices, or toast rounds, for serving	

* Carefully pick over crab or lobster to ensure that no shell or cartilage remains.

Using small saucepan, sprinkle gelatin over lemon juice. Let stand 1 minute to soften, then warm over low heat, stirring until gelatin dissolves. Set aside.

In food processor combine half of shrimp, cream cheese, salmon, crab, vegetables, dill, ketchup, cayenne and ½ cup/125 mL sour cream. Process until smooth. Season with salt, if desired, and pepper.

Line 9 inch/1 L springform pan with plastic wrap. Pour in mixture; cover and refrigerate at least 2 hours (or overnight).

To serve, place large serving platter over springform pan, holding both tips upside down, then remove pan and carefully remove plastic wrap. Spread remaining sour cream in centre of mousse. Top with reserved shrimp and garnish.

Serves 8 to 10.

Note: I didn't want to dig out my springform pan, so I used a shallow bowl and allowed the wrap to overlap the sides. When the mousse is inverted, give it a couple of gentle tugs and it should come out just fine.

Oyster Shooter

One day I rashly promised Lars Davidson, a budding screenwriter, that I would include his recipe in my next book. He claims it's a drink some people rave about. So here it is, Lars.

"Shuck 1 raw oyster and put in shooter or wine glass. Top with ½ oz/15 mL white wine (sweetness of 7 or more), sprinkling of ginger root and Italian seasoning, pinch of garlic and small chunk of Danish blue cheese. Swish ingredients around in glass, and down the hatch!"

Makes 1 shooter.

Lobster Pie

This recipe is perfect for enjoying the European tradition of packing a pie for a picnic. For safety, follow the adage of "keep it hot or keep it cold, but never in-between," when picnicking. This pie is a wonderful dinner selection as well, as it requires only a salad or vegetable to make a complete meal.

1	pastry for double crust pie (use your own recipe, adding pinch garlic salt, cayenne pepper, freshly ground pepper, and tbsp dried parsley)	1
¼ cup	Parmesan cheese	60 mL
½ cup	mushrooms, sliced	125 mL
½ cup	green onions, sliced	125 mL
½	yellow pepper, chopped fairly fine (optional)	½
2 cups	lobster meat, drained and chopped	500 mL
2	large eggs	2
⅔ cup	milk	160 mL
¼ cup	dry white wine	60 mL
¼ cup	fresh parsley, chopped	60 mL
	Black pepper, freshly ground, to taste	
¼ tsp	nutmeg	1 mL
½	lemon, zest of	½

Preheat oven to 400°F/200°C. Prepare pastry in deep or straight-sided dish. Sprinkle layer of cheese onto pastry. Layer mushrooms, onion, yellow pepper and lobster until used up. Arrange so that filling is dense and without spaces.

Place remaining ingredients in blender and process until smooth. Pour over lobster, just until covered; do not overfill. Cover with pastry, sealing sides well and crimping. Slit to allow steam to escape.

Bake at 400°F/200°C for 15 minutes then reduce heat to 350°F/180°C for about 30 minutes, or until skewer inserted in middle of pie comes out clean. Cool on rack.

Serves 4 to 6.

For the Love of Pizza

Pizza is an integral part of life for us. We love the easy eating, delicious flavours and sense of informal socializing that go with a good pizza. I suggest that you experiment with types of pizza and cheese blends until you get one or two down pat, then keep those ingredients on hand so that you can whip up a pizza any time company drops in. For instance, we buy cheeses in bulk and shred them in the food processor when we get home. The cheese goes further, and makes fast preparation a snap. Do it often enough and you will develop a "signature pizza" — a combination that people come to associate with you, and you alone. To make your first efforts easier, shop at a deli and ask for exactly the weight of each cheese needed.

White Cheese Seafood Pizza

Pizza prepared with no sauce, commonly called "white cheese pizza" is receiving rave reviews because the cheeses don't have to blend well with tomato sauce. Experimenting with different cheese blends can produce delicious results. Blends should feature a combination of soft cheeses, for a smooth melt that covers the crust and other ingredients, and firm cheeses that provide body and full flavour.

1	pre-made, uncooked 12 inch/30 cm pizza crust	1
4 oz	seafood, such as uncooked shrimp, sole or halibut, cut into bite-size pieces	125 g
3 oz	Havarti cheese, grated	90 g
3 oz	Bel Paese cheese, grated	90 g
1 oz	Blue cheese, crumbled	30 g

Spread seafood on pizza dough, followed by shredded Havarti and Bel Paese. Top with crumbled Blue cheese. Bake at 400°F/200°C until melted and slightly browned.

Serves 2 to 4.

Salmon & Artichoke Pizza

When I first tried this, it called for a crust made using frozen bread dough. Although we often buy a pre-prepared crust at the supermarket, for this recipe I prefer a high quality homemade pizza base to match the elegance of the toppings. Serve with a traditional Caesar or spinach salad.

½ cup	sour cream	125 mL
2 tsp	Dijon mustard	10 mL
1 tsp	dried dillweed	5 mL
	or 1 tbsp/15 mL fresh dillweed, chopped	
2½ cups	Swiss cheese, grated	625 mL
¼ lb	smoked salmon, sliced into thin strips	125 g
1	can (14 oz/398 mL) artichoke hearts, drained and dried on paper towels	1
	or medium-size leek, trimmed, cleaned and sliced crosswise, about ¼ inch/0.5 cm thick	
2	green onions, including tops, chopped	2
1 tbsp	capers	15 mL
1	high quality, 12 inch/30 cm pizza base	1

In large bowl blend sour cream, mustard and dill. Stir in 1½ cups/375 mL cheese and set aside.

Smooth cheese mixture evenly over pizza crust. Top with salmon, artichokes or leeks, onions and capers. Sprinkle remaining cheese over top. Bake according to directions that accompany pizza crust. Serve hot.

Serves 6 to 8.

Classic Red Sauce Pizza with Crab

Pizza chefs have been using variations on this classic cheese blend for years. Mozzarella and Provolone provide perfect melt and stretch characteristics. Whole milk Mozzarella lends a soft, creamy texture, Provolone adds full flavour, and the sharp taste of a well-aged Cheddar rounds out the three cheese combination. If you use coloured (orange) cheddar, you will have a darker colour pizza, especially if the cheddar is placed on top of the cheese blend. This blend is so flavourful that it's ideally suited to simple cheese pizzas, but we like to add luscious seafood and perhaps a few veggies.

1	pre-made, uncooked 12 inch/30 cm pizza crust	1
	Tomato sauce*, enough to cover dough	
4-5 oz	flaked crab meat, drained well	125-155 g
2	green onions, sliced	2
¼ cup	yellow pepper, diced	60 mL
2 oz	Mozzarella, grated	60 g
2 oz	mild Provolone, grated	60 g
3 oz	sharp Cheddar cheese, grated	90 g

* The tomato sauce you use is a personal choice — we use some of the reduced-fat, chunky spaghetti sauces and love them.

Spread tomato sauce on dough to within ½ inch/1.25 cm of edge. Top with crab, onion, pepper, Mozzarella, Provolone and then Cheddar. Bake 10 to 15 minutes at 400°F/200°C, until golden brown.

Serves 2 to 4.

Jack's Best with Lobster

This cheese blend is full flavoured but mild. It is also firmer to the bite and has less stretch than a traditional blend, and it will brown more than Mozzarella. We like this combination with lobster, but urge you to develop your own favourite.

1	pre-made, uncooked 12 inch/30 cm pizza crust	1
	Tomato sauce*, enough to cover dough	
4-5 oz	pre-cooked lobster meat, drained well, chopped (reserve claws for garnish)	125-155 g
3 oz	Mozzarella (low-moisture, part skim), grated	90 g
3 oz	mild Cheddar, grated	90 g
2 oz	Monterey Jack, grated	60 g

* Use your tomato sauce of choice.

Spread tomato sauce on dough to within ½ inch/1.25 cm of edge; add lobster and cheeses and bake 10 to 15 minutes at 400°F/200°C, until golden brown.

Serves 2 to 4.

Oriental Salmon Braid

Here is a mouth-watering treat that can be made before guests arrive, then refrigerated for an hour or so until you are ready to cook. The exotic mayonnaise mixture of salmon, rice and savoury Chinese flavours, wrapped in a golden puff pastry, is a sure-fire pleaser — great to serve at half-time if you have friends in to watch a game on TV, or as a snack after cards.

1	pkg (7 ½ oz/213 g) frozen puff pastry, thawed	1
1	can (7 ½ oz/213 g) salmon	1
½ cup	long grain rice, cooked	125 mL
¼ cup	green onion, chopped	60 mL
¼ cup	water chestnuts, sliced	60 mL
1 tsp	garlic powder	5 mL
¼ cup	bean sprouts	60 mL
1½ tsp	fresh ginger, grated	7 mL
1 tbsp	soy sauce	15 mL
2½ tsp	Hoisin sauce	12 mL
⅓ cup	mayonnaise	80 mL
Dash	black pepper, ground	Dash
1	egg, well beaten	1

Roll out pastry on floured board, into square 12x12 inches/30x30 cm. Combine salmon, its juices, well-mashed bones and all remaining ingredients except egg. Mix well and spread down centre ⅓ of pastry square. Leave ⅓ pastry uncovered on each side of filling.

Using sharp, unserrated knife, cut slits diagonally from filling to outer edges of pastry on either side of filling. Make slits about 1½ to 2 inches/3.75 to 5 cm apart. Lift resulting pastry strips and alternately braid them across top of filling. With beaten egg, seal edges and brush finished braid. Refrigerate while preheating oven to 400°F/200°C. Bake about 20 minutes or until golden brown.

Serves 4 to 6.

Microwaved Shell-On Shrimp
with Dippers

One of the best ways to loosen up guests is to involve them with their food. If they share bowls of dipping sauce, they just have to talk to each other. Don't forget to put out bowls for shells, and lots of napkins.

1 lb	raw shrimp, shell on	500 g
	Dips (recipes follow)	

Spread 1 lb/500 g raw, shell-on shrimp evenly on flat platter, 1 layer deep. Add splash of water. Leave round hole in middle. Cover tightly with clear plastic wrap. Microwave on high for 2 minutes; turn plate and cook for another 1 to 2½ minutes. Let stand for 2 minutes, then remove to hot serving bowl or platter.

While first batch is cooking, you can cook a second. Let guests help themselves and peel their own shrimp, dipping them in commercially prepared dips such as seafood sauce, or the two homemade dips that follow.

Teriyaki Dipping Sauce:

⅓ cup	light soy sauce	80 mL
3 tbsp	sherry	45 mL
2 tbsp	honey	30 mL
1	clove garlic, finely minced	1
1½ tsp	fresh ginger, finely grated	7 mL
1	green onion, thinly sliced	1

Combine ingredients and serve.

Tarragon Mayonnaise:

½ cup	low-fat mayonnaise	125 mL
1 tbsp	fresh lemon juice	15 mL
1 tsp	dried tarragon	5 mL
1 tsp	Dijon mustard	5 mL

Combine ingredients and chill ½ hour before serving.

Between Two Slices

Sandwiches

Now that grain foods such as breads are widely known to be healthy and nutritious as well as delicious, sandwiches are making a comeback. They have, however, taken on a new look. Today's sandwich combines different ingredients, piles on loads of veggies, can be open-faced and often makes a meal in itself.

Finnan Haddie Benedict

Since I associate Finnan Haddie, or smoked cod, with breakfast and don't particularly like the dried-up bits of ham that restaurants seem to serve, it was natural that this variation of Eggs Benedict would appeal to me. Hollandaise can be made from scratch, from a packaged mix or procured from a can. Allow 1 muffin per person.

Smoked cod fillets (measure quantity according to number of muffins you will be topping)

English muffins (1 per person), split, toasted and buttered

Spinach (1½ tbsp/20 mL per person), cooked

Eggs (1 per muffin half), poached

Hollandaise sauce

Paprika

Cut fillets into portions that will nicely fit on top of muffin halves. Poach in water or milk. On each muffin, layer 1½ tbsp/20 mL spinach and portion of cod; add poached egg. Spoon 1½ tbsp/20 mL hollandaise over each egg. Sprinkle with paprika and serve.

The Melt

Tuna melts are a favourite from my teens. We used to toast English muffins, apply a daub of tuna mixed with mayo, a slice of tomato and a slice of cheese, and pop them under the broiler. The concept remains, but today we use many different seafoods such as crab, lobster, salmon and, of course, tuna, and we've fancied things up just a little. Look for the Mexican Melt variation that follows and let it become a stimulus for your creativity — invent your own "melts" and enjoy.

1 cup	(or 7½ oz/213 g can) seafood, such as tuna lobster, crab or salmon	250 mL
2 tbsp	green onion, chopped	30 mL
2 tbsp	green pepper, chopped	30 mL
3 tbsp	mayonnaise	45 mL
	Salt and pepper, to taste	
2	bagels, English muffins, kaisers or other buns, cut in half horizontally and toasted	2
8	slices tomato	8
4	slices red onion	4
8	slices Monterey Jack or Swiss cheese	8

Combine tuna, green onion, green pepper, mayonnaise, salt and pepper. Place on bun halves and top with tomato, onion and cheese slices. Bake 5 to 7 minutes in 350°F/180°C oven; then place under broiler to brown.

Serves 2.

Variation: The Mexican Melt
Vary the amount of jalapeño pepper to achieve either a mildly piquant touch or a fiery effect, and garnish with a dollop of sour cream.

1 cup	(or 7½ oz/213 g can) salmon (or other ready-to-eat seafood), drained	250 mL
¼ cup	Cheddar cheese, grated	60 mL
¼ cup	Monterey Jack cheese, grated	60 mL
1 tsp	(or quantity to taste) jalapeño peppers, finely chopped	5 mL
1 tsp	Worcestershire sauce	5 mL
3	English muffins, split in half	3
Pinch	paprika	Pinch
	Sour cream, for garnish	

Flake salmon and mash bones. Combine with cheese, peppers and Worcestershire sauce. Divide between muffin halves. Sprinkle with paprika. Broil until cheese is melted and muffins start to brown. Garnish with sour cream.

Serves 3.

Santa Fe Hot Crab Meat Sandwich

The Southwest United States is having an influence on everything from interior decorating to art and fashion. Nowhere is the impact more visible than in cuisine. At times the influence is subtle — the addition of hot sauce or chilies to a hot sandwich such as this, which is a hit at the *Pink Adobe* in Santa Fe, New Mexico.

1	clove garlic, minced	1
1 tbsp	olive oil	15 mL
1 cup	fresh or frozen flaked crab meat, picked free of shell and cartilage	250 mL
1	egg	1
1 tbsp	cream	15 mL
Dash	salt	Dash
Dash	cayenne	Dash
¼ tsp	Tabasco sauce	1 mL
2	buns, buttered and toasted	2

Sauté garlic in olive oil. Add crab meat and mix well. Keep warm. In mixing bowl, beat egg gently and stir in cream, salt, cayenne, and Tabasco. Stir very slowly and gently into hot crab meat and cook over low heat. Do not stop stirring gently until mixture is light and egg has set. Spread on toasted, buttered buns at once.

Serves 2.

Crab Rolls Alaskan Style

Two things all "foodies" associate with Alaska — crab and sourdough bread — are combined in this fabulous sandwich, which is prepared with savoury capers and crunchy scallions. If you can't find or make sourdough rolls, make this sandwich on sourdough bread or spoon into another type of roll.

2 tbsp	ketchup	30 mL
¼ cup	sour cream	60 mL
¼ cup	mayonnaise	60 mL
⅛ cup	scallions or green onions, thinly sliced	30 mL
2 tsp	Worcestershire sauce	10 mL
2 tsp	capers	10 mL
	Salt and pepper, to taste	
1 lb	crab meat, fresh or frozen, picked clean of shell and cartilage	500 g
8	leaves Boston lettuce	8
4	sourdough rolls	4

In bowl combine ketchup, sour cream and mayonnaise. Add remaining ingredients, except lettuce and rolls. Lightly toast rolls. Line with lettuce and divide crab meat mixture between them.

Serves 4 (1 each).

Mexican Style Lobster Pockets

Here's a south of the border sensation: tortillas stuffed with lobster, veggies and cheese, with an extra kick provided by homemade Jalapeño Mayo. You can speed up preparation time by mixing regular mayonnaise with mustard, pepper and jalapeño pepper, but we can't guarantee that it will be as good!

4	large flour tortillas or large pita breads	4
1	avocado, cubed	1
½-¾ cup	lobster meat, cut into small pieces	125-180 mL
4 oz	Monterey Jack cheese, cubed	125 g
	Alfalfa sprouts	
¼ cup	black olives, pitted and halved	60 mL
5	cherry tomatoes, quartered	5
	Jalapeño Mayo (recipe follows)	

Preheat oven to 400°F/200°C. Wrap tortillas or pitas in foil and warm in oven 7 to 10 minutes. In bowl combine avocado, lobster, cheese, alfalfa sprouts, olives and tomatoes. Spread 1 tbsp/15 mL Jalapeño Mayo in centre of each tortilla or pita. Spoon filling into tortillas or pitas, dividing evenly. Fold sides of tortillas inward to form pockets. Serve.

Serves 4 (1 each).

Jalapeño Mayo:

1	large egg yolk	1
½ tsp	lemon juice	2 mL
½ tsp	white-wine vinegar	2 mL
½ tsp	dry mustard	2 mL
½ tsp	salt	2 mL
10	grinds black pepper	10
1 cup	oil	250 mL
1 tsp	jalapeño pepper, finely chopped	5 mL

Whisk together first 6 ingredients. Then very slowly whisk in oil, until it is all incorporated. Add jalapeño pepper and mix thoroughly.

Cajun Tacos

Every so often it pays to take notice of what the kids are doing. I kept seeing them buy these taco things, and wondering how anyone can enjoy them. Well, I tried this version and was hooked. Vary the fillings, if you like — other seafoods such as lobster and smoked salmon work wonderfully well. This recipe makes enough for a party or informal gathering — and they're also great for teenagers tucking in after a morning hockey game, or tumbling home after basketball or swimming. For a reduced-calorie offering, serve the egg mixture enchilada-style, in a warm flour tortilla or stuffed in a heated pita pocket.

1	yellow pepper, diced	1
2	medium red onions, diced	2
¼ cup	water	60 mL
16	eggs	16
½ cup	plain 1% yogurt	125 mL
1 tbsp	Worcestershire sauce	15 mL
¼ cup	chives, chopped	60 mL
5 oz	baby shrimp (canned are fine)	155 g
12	taco shells	12
	Alfalfa sprouts	
2	tomatoes, diced	2
¾ cup	chunky salsa	180 mL

Combine peppers, onions and water in large non-stick skillet. Cook until vegetables are just tender and moisture evaporates. Beat eggs with yogurt, Worcestershire sauce and chives. Add to vegetables and cook until eggs begin to set. Add shrimp and continue cooking and stirring until eggs are set — they should look like scrambled eggs. Don't overcook.

Line taco shells with alfalfa sprouts and tomato. Fill each with egg mixture and top with 1 tbsp/15 mL salsa. When feeding a crowd, pop tacos into warm oven as you make them so that platter can be taken out all at once.

Makes 12 tacos.

Danish Open-Faced Sandwich

The Danish open-faced sandwich is gaining popularity in North America. Start with bread — whole grain, rye, pumpernickel or coarse white — that is buttered or spread with flavoured cream cheese. Top it with more cheese and garnishes such as smoked or pickled fish.

Here is one to get you started: rye, butter, Havarti cheese, smoked sturgeon and a tomato rose.

And another: caviar with cream cheese, egg salad and smoked fish, or simply a slice of tomato and sprig of watercress.

Open-Faced Troutwich

This is a variation of the "melt." I've included it to show the variety you can attain with just a little experimenting. It's also a yummy way to use up leftover cooked fish.

2 cups	cooked trout, flaked, bones removed	500 mL
⅓ cup	mayonnaise	80 mL
2 tbsp	celery, finely chopped	30 mL
2 tbsp	mushrooms, finely chopped	30 mL
2 tsp	prepared mustard	10 mL
1 tbsp	onion, finely chopped (optional)	15 mL
	Black pepper, freshly ground, to taste	
6	slices dark rye, or other bread, toasted	6
6	slices Gruyere cheese	6
6	slices tomato	6

Combine first 7 ingredients; spread on toast. Top each with tomato slice. Broil 2 minutes. Remove and top each with slice of Gruyere cheese. Return to broiler until cheese melts, 2 to 3 minutes.

Serves 3 to 6.

Smoked Trout with Mustard-Dill Sauce

It seems that every town has a bakery that sells delicious cheese buns or scones. Team them up with smoked trout and this sauce for a delicious treat. I toast mine because I like everything better toasted, but it isn't necessary to do so. Serve open-faced or as a sandwich.

3	cheese buns or scones, split horizontally, and lightly buttered if desired	3
6	thin slices smoked trout	6
	Mustard-Dill Sauce (recipe follows)	
	Fresh dill sprigs	

Top each bun or scone with slice of trout. Spoon some sauce over top and garnish with dill sprigs.

Mustard-Dill Sauce:

2 tbsp	Dijon mustard	30 mL
1 tbsp	sugar	15 mL
1 tbsp	white wine vinegar	15 mL
½ tsp	dry mustard	2 mL
¼ cup	vegetable oil	60 mL
2 tbsp	fresh dill, chopped	30 mL

Combine Dijon mustard, sugar, vinegar and dry mustard in food processor or blender. With machine running, add oil in thin stream through feed tube. Add chopped dill and mix until sauce thickens to mayonnaise consistency, stopping to scrape down sides of bowl as necessary. Cover and refrigerate until ready to use.

Serves 2 to 3.

Fisherman's Delight

¼ tsp	cracked black pepper	1 mL
1 tbsp	light or salad oil	15 mL
1 tbsp	Dijon mustard, with seeds	15 mL
2 tsp	white wine vinegar	10 mL
Pinch	salt (optional)	Pinch
4	catfish fillets (about 1 lb/500 g)	4
1½ cups	dark romaine lettuce, shredded	375 mL
½ cup	radishes, grated	125 mL
1	small carrot, grated	1
½	small yellow pepper, very thinly sliced	½
	Dressing (recipe follows)	
4	8-inch/20-cm sub, poor boy or hoagie rolls, cut in half horizontally	4

About 30 minutes before serving, combine black pepper, oil, mustard, vinegar and pinch of salt (if desired) in pie plate or flat dish big enough to lay out fillets. Place fillets in marinade, turning to coat. Set aside for ½ hour.

Preheat broiler. Put fillets on rack in broiling pan. Place close to heat and broil 5 to 7 minutes, brushing occasionally with remaining marinade. Combine romaine lettuce, radish, carrot and yellow pepper. Add dressing to mixture, tossing well. Divide mix between 4 rolls; top with catfish fillets and remaining roll.

Serves 4.

Dressing:

2 tbsp	salad or light oil	30 mL
2 tsp	white wine vinegar	10 mL
½ tsp	mustard	2 mL
¼ tsp	salt	1 mL
¼ tsp	sugar	1 mL
⅛ tsp	celery seeds	0.5 mL

Combine ingredients in cup, mixing well with fork.

Grilled Salmon Sandwiches

This open-faced sandwich recipe was in my Weight Watchers file with the big red heart that I use to signify "I love it." Grill the salmon on your outdoor BBQ or under the broiler. The reason this is a "low-cal" recipe is that you are controlling the fat content of the sauce and getting flavour in a healthy way.

4	(3 oz/90 g) salmon fillets, without skin	4
1 tbsp	fresh tarragon, minced *or* ½ tsp/2 mL dried tarragon	15 mL
¼ tsp	pepper, freshly ground	1 mL
¼ tsp	salt	1 mL
2	garlic cloves, minced	2
2 tsp	olive oil	10 mL
¼ cup	chicken broth (low-sodium, if possible)	60 mL
1 tbsp	sweet pickle relish	15 mL
2 tsp	lemon juice	10 mL
Pinch	ground red pepper	Pinch
1	English cucumber, thinly sliced	1
2	tomatoes, sliced	2
8	slices bread, toasted	8
	Non-stick cooking spray	

Spray grill with non-stick cooking spray and heat barbecue or oven to medium heat. Sprinkle both sides of salmon with tarragon, pepper and salt. Grill until cooked (about 5 minutes each side).

While cooking, prepare sauce: sauté garlic in oil, stirring for about 2 minutes over medium-high heat. Add broth, relish, lemon juice and red pepper. Cook, stirring constantly until sauce boils and reduces slightly (about 3 minutes). Remove from heat.

Assemble sandwich by layering cucumber, tomato, salmon fillet and drizzle of sauce. Best eaten warm when you can really savour grilled flavour.

Serves 4.

Downright Healthy Pacific Club

The Club Sandwich is an integral part of our culinary history — turkey, bacon, cheese, lettuce, tomato, all slathered with mayo. If you love the concept but want to be more health-conscious, try this variation on the Club. If you want to add a little kick, shred some radish in place of the carrot. We prefer to toast the bread, but the sandwich is fine either way.

1	can (7½ oz/213 g) salmon or tuna, drained	1
¼ cup	non-cholesterol mayonnaise	60 mL
2 tsp	lemon juice	10 mL
	Pepper, to taste	
6	slices wholewheat, multi-grain or light bread, toasted and lightly buttered	6
	Alfalfa sprouts	
1	cucumber, peeled and thinly sliced	1
1	tomato, sliced	1
1	carrot, finely shredded	1

Mash seafood, including any bones, with mayonnaise, lemon juice and pepper to taste. Top 2 slices toast with salmon and cucumber. On top of each slice place another slice toast with sprinkle of shredded carrot, tomato slices and alfalfa sprouts. Top each again with third slice of bread. Cut into quarters and hold together with toothpick.

Makes 2 sandwiches.

Oven "Fried" Salmon Burgers

A Home Economist sent me this recipe when I was writing a cookbook for the Heart and Stroke Foundation. She said it was perfect because it doesn't require adding extra fat in the preparation or cooking. The recipe came too late for that book, so we can benefit from it here. These patties can be assembled or baked a day ahead and refrigerated until ready to use. Naked patties can be reheated, covered, in the microwave or oven. We also discovered they make a great "sandwich" when raiding the fridge for leftovers. I always make extra to enjoy in lunches the next day — if you like them hot, just zap them in the microwave to warm.

2	egg whites from large eggs *or* 1 whole large egg	2
1	can (15 oz/425 g) salmon, drained and flaked	1
1 cup	fresh breadcrumbs	250 mL
¼ cup	green onions, finely chopped	60 mL
¼ cup	celery, finely chopped	60 mL
2 tbsp	fresh lemon juice	30 mL
1 tsp	Worcestershire sauce	5 mL
	Whole or multi-grain rolls, split	
	Non-stick cooking spray	
	Alfalfa or radish sprouts	
	Tomato slices	
	Calorie-reduced ranch dressing	

Preheat oven to 400°F/200°C. Spray cookie sheet with non-stick cooking spray. Beat egg with fork; add salmon, breadcrumbs, green onions, celery, lemon juice and Worcestershire sauce, mixing until well blended.

Shape into 8 ½-inch/1.25-cm thick patties. Place on cookie sheet and bake 10 to 12 minutes, turning once, until golden brown on both sides. Spread a little dressing on bottom of roll, add salmon patty, sprouts and tomato, and enjoy.

Serves 4 to 8.

Reuben Sandwich Mariner's Style

A chef at the Culinary Institute of Canada gave me this recipe and told me never to reveal that it was his favourite fish dish. This recipe makes eight portions, so adjust it to the number of people you are serving.

8	slices rye bread	8
	Butter	
3 tbsp	Russian salad dressing	45 mL
8	fish portions, breaded and baked according to directions	8
1 cup	sauerkraut, well drained	250 mL
	Swiss cheese	

Butter bread (you may wish to toast it first) and sprinkle with salad dressing. Place fish portion on each slice, then cover with sauerkraut and sliced Swiss cheese. Broil until cheese is melted and bubbly.

Serves 4 to 8.

Oyster Po'boy

The po'boy is as much a part of a visit to Louisiana as visits to the New Orleans French Quarter. The actual presentation varies from establishment to establishment, but the one common denominator seems to be the French bread and the oysters. This recipe is a combination of one from the great chef Paul Prudhomme and another I found in my files. Make up the seasoning mix and mayonnaise before you start cooking.

	Seasoning Mix (recipe follows)	
16 oz	oysters*, shucked	500 g
½ cup	all purpose flour	125 mL
½ cup	corn flour**	125 mL
½ cup	cornmeal	125 mL
2	long French loaves	2
4 tbsp	unsalted butter	60 mL
	Garlic Mayonnaise (recipe follows)	
	Vegetable oil, for deep-frying	
	Iceberg lettuce, shredded	

* Oysters removed from the shell are available at most seafood retailers, in tubs or jars. If not available, purchase enough to feed 4 and shuck your own.

** Available at natural food stores, or make your own by finely grinding ½ cup/125 mL corn meal in food processor or blender.

In medium bowl, stir 1 tbsp/15 mL seasoning mix into undrained oysters. Marinate for 2 hours at room temperature. Blend together flour, corn flour, cornmeal and remaining seasoning mixture in second bowl.

Cut top third off bread horizontally. Remove some bread from inside of bottom half to form shell. Lightly butter inside of shell and "lid." Lightly toast under broiler, then spread with generous portion of Garlic Mayonnaise.

Thoroughly drain oysters, discarding liquor. Heat at least 3 inches/7.5 cm oil in deep-fryer or wok, to approximately 375°F/190°C. Dredge oysters one at a time in flour mixture. Shake off excess flour and slip into hot oil a few at a time (be careful not to crowd oysters as this will slow cooking and oysters will stick together). Fry until crisp and float to surface, about 1 minute. Remove to paper towels and drain well. Always allow fat to come back up to temperature before starting next batch.

Keep oysters warm until all are cooked, then fill hollowed-out bread with them; top with shredded lettuce and lid of bread. Gently drop loaves on flat surface to compact oysters and lettuce. Serve with remaining Garlic Mayonnaise, cutting into sections about 7 inches/18 cm long.

Serves 4.

See over for Seasoning Mix and Garlic Mayonnaise.

Seasoning Mix:

2¼ tsp	salt	11 mL
¾ tsp	garlic powder	3 mL
¾ tsp	Hungarian sweet paprika	3 mL
½ tsp	onion powder	2 mL
½ tsp	ground red pepper (cayenne)	2 mL
½ tsp	pepper, freshly ground	2 mL
½ tsp	dried oregano, crumbled	2 mL
¼ tsp	white pepper, freshly ground	1 mL
¼ tsp	dried thyme, crumbled	1 mL
⅛ tsp	dried basil, crumbled	0.5 mL

Combine all ingredients in jar or small bowl.

Garlic Mayonnaise:

2½ tbsp	fresh garlic, minced	35 mL
2 tbsp	unsalted butter	30 mL
2 tbsp	onion, minced	30 mL
1 tbsp	fresh lemon juice	15 mL
½ tsp	salt	2 mL
½ tsp	hot pepper sauce (optional)	2 mL
¼ tsp	white pepper, freshly ground	1 mL
¼ tsp	cayenne pepper	1 mL
1	egg, at room temperature	1
1	egg yolk, at room temperature	1
2 cups	vegetable oil	500 mL

Combine first 8 ingredients in heavy 1½ qt/1.5 L saucepan. Sauté over medium-low heat until vegetables soften, about 4 minutes. Cool 15 minutes.

Mix egg and yolk in processor or blender for 30 seconds. Add vegetable mixture and purée about 15 seconds. With machine running, slowly add oil through feed tube. Stop machine and scrape down sides. Continue mixing until mayonnaise is thick and creamy, about 15 seconds. Cover and refrigerate at least 30 minutes.

Hearty Eating

Soups, Stews & Chowders

Here's "comfort food" at its best, with some new twists on old favourites: soups, stews and chowders. More than just delicious, these recipes are nutritious and satisfying — and they're among the best ways to stretch your seafood dollars.

Seafood Stew Poupon Dijon

Picture a bowl heaped with steaming seafood, nestled amongst clams and mussels in their shells, all in a rich golden broth. You have it! As with our Bouillabaisse, you can prepare this stew ahead of time up to the stage where you add fish. If you are serving fewer than ten, adjust the amount of seafood accordingly and freeze the unused stock for later use.

3 lb	firm-fleshed fish, cut into chunks	1.5 kg
40	fresh clams or mussels in the shell	40
30	shrimp, peeled and deveined	30
20	tiny new potatoes	20
1½ lb	onions, sliced	750 g
5	garlic cloves, minced	5
5	leeks, white only, sliced (if large, use 4)	5
3 oz	olive oil	90 mL
4	large ripe tomatoes, seeded and chopped	4
1 cup	Dijon mustard	250 mL
1½	bay leaves	1½
¾ tsp	dried thyme	3 mL
¼ cup	fresh parsley, chopped	60 mL
¼ tsp	dried rosemary	1 mL
¼ tsp	dried fennel	1 mL
1 tbsp	orange juice concentrate *or* 2 tsp/10 mL grated orange rind	15 mL
1¾ qt	fish stock	1.75 L
	Salt (omit if using prepared fish stock), to taste	
	Pepper, to taste	
	Zest of orange, to garnish	

Prepare seafood by washing shells of clams or mussels. Scrub new potatoes and put on stove to boil so that they will be ready at same time as stew.

Sauté onions, garlic and leek in olive oil until tender. Add tomatoes, Dijon mustard, spices, seasonings and orange juice concentrate; simmer 5 minutes.

Add fish stock; simmer 5 minutes; season with salt and pepper. (If preparing for less than 10 people, pour off portion of stock and freeze.)

Add fish, clams or mussels and simmer covered for 5 minutes. Add shrimp and simmer until clams open. Spoon into serving bowls, making sure everyone has some of each seafood. Add 2 new potatoes to each serving and sprinkle with orange zest.

Serves 10.

Sea-Noodle Soup

One of the best places to find new, innovative recipes and get meal ideas is from food producers. The original for this one came from *Catelli*. Many combinations of seafood will work in this soup, such as a mixture of cubed orange roughy fillets, scallops and cooked shrimp. Check out the chowder mix at your seafood counter — it is often a "best buy."

5 cups	chicken broth	1.25 L
1 tbsp	soy sauce	15 mL
2	cloves garlic, minced	2
1 tsp	fresh ginger root, finely chopped	5 mL
½ tsp	dried red pepper, crushed	2 mL
¼	pkg (14 oz/375 g) fine egg noodles	¼
¾ lb	fresh white fish fillets, cubed	375 g
2	green onions, chopped	2
1 tbsp	lime juice	15 mL

In saucepan, bring broth and soy sauce to boil. Stir in garlic, ginger root, crushed red pepper and noodles. Simmer 6 minutes.

Add fish; simmer 3 minutes longer or until fish is opaque. Stir in green onions and lime juice.

Serves 6.

Mediterranean Fennel Seafood Stew

H ere is a delicious dish that is both nourishing and low in fat.

2¼ cups	water	560 mL
2 cups	dry white wine	500 mL
1 tbsp	thyme	15 mL
3	bay leaves	3
2	fennel bulbs, leaves trimmed off	2
2	pinches saffron	2
1 lb	large shrimp, peeled and deveined	500 g
4 lb	mussels	2 kg
4	cloves garlic, crushed	4
1 lb	sea scallops	500 g
1 lb	monkfish, cut into 2-inch/5-cm cubes	500 g
3	firm, ripe tomatoes, coarsely chopped	3
2 tbsp	parsley, freshly chopped	30 mL

In saucepan large enough to hold both fennel bulbs, boil 1 cup/250 mL water and 1 cup/250 mL wine. Add 1 tsp/5 mL thyme and 1 bay leaf and steam fennel bulb 5 to 10 minutes, depending on size, until just tender. Remove from liquid and slice lengthwise. Add pinch of saffron to cooling liquid and set aside.

In second saucepan, boil 1 cup/250 mL water and ¾ cup/180 mL wine. Add 1 tsp/5 mL thyme, bay leaf and shrimp. Cook 2 to 3 minutes, until shrimp turn pink but remain firm. Remove shrimp and reserve broth. Steam mussels using ¼ cup/60 mL water, remaining wine, thyme, bay leaf and garlic. Cook, covered, until shells open. Transfer mussels to bowl, discarding any that did not open. Strain broth through coffee filter or cheesecloth.

About 10 minutes before serving, combine broths in broad-based pot or deep skillet and bring to boil. Add scallops and monkfish and poach for about 5 minutes. Add tomatoes, parsley, mussels, shrimp and fennel; continue cooking until all ingredients are heated through. Serve immediately.

Serves 6 to 8.

Lobster Bisque

If you are making this bisque as part of a lobster feast, reserve the claw and tail meat for other presentations and make the bisque with broken or small meat pieces. Two lobsters serve four to six people.

2	medium-size lobsters, boiled without salt	2
2½ cups	chicken stock	625 mL
1	onion, sliced	1
3-4	whole stalks celery	3-4
2	whole cloves	2
1	bay leaf	1
6	peppercorns	6
¼ cup	butter	60 mL
¼ cup	flour	60 mL
¼ tsp	nutmeg	1 mL
3 cups	hot milk	750 mL
1 cup	cream	250 mL
Dash	paprika	Dash
	Dry sherry, if desired	
	Parsley or other fresh herb, for garnish	

Remove meat from lobster, picking shells clean. Crush shells and place in stock pot with chicken stock, onion, celery, cloves, bay leaf and peppercorns. Simmer for 2 ½ hours, then drain, reserving stock.

Meanwhile, finely chop lobster meat. Any coral roe should be mixed with butter (to do this, force roe through sieve, then mix butter and roe until well blended). Melt butter mixture; add flour and nutmeg; blend well. Gradually add heated milk, stirring until sauce is smooth and just boiling. Gently add lobster and stock, simmering another 5 minutes.

Heat (but don't boil) cream. Remove from heat and stir cream into bisque. Add paprika. Adjust seasonings, using a little dry sherry, if desired. Garnish with chopped parsley or fresh herb.

Serves 4 to 6.

Atlantic Canadian Bouillabaisse

The famous Mediterranean fisherman's stew takes on a unique Canadian flavour when made with the abundant seafoods of the Atlantic coast. Lobster is the featured ingredient, adding colour and its wonderfully distinctive flavour to this visually pleasing, exceptionally tasty combination of seafood simmered in a heady, herb-seasoned broth. Serve it as a one-dish meal for two, and it will bring a glow of romance to the table.

2 tbsp	butter	30 mL
2 tbsp	oil	30 mL
2	large leeks, chopped	2
1	onion, chopped	1
1	large carrot, chopped	1
2	stalks celery, chopped	2
4	cloves garlic, minced	4
3	ripe tomatoes, peeled and chopped (or use canned)	3
½ tsp	saffron, crushed	2 mL
¼ tsp	dried tarragon or fennel seeds, crushed	1 mL
½ tsp	dried thyme, crushed	2 mL
8-12 oz	dry white wine	250-375 mL
6 cups	good Fish Stock (recipe follows)	1.5 L
	Salt and pepper, to taste	
2	whole lobster (approximately ¾ lb/375 g each), frozen in brine, thawed and drained*	2
6	scallops	6
4	clams	4
10	mussels	10
1	thick fillet or slice salmon, uncooked	1
1	thick fillet or slice firm white fish (halibut, haddock, turbot, or cod), uncooked	1
	Parsley, chopped	

* Lobster can be left whole, to serve 1 each, or chopped into pieces. If leaving whole, carefully crack shell prior to cooking to allow for easy removal of meat from claws, knuckles and tail. Cracking or chopping into pieces will allow seasoning to penetrate meat.

In large, heavy pot, melt butter with oil. Add leeks, onion, carrot, celery and garlic. Cook until softened. Add tomatoes, saffron, tarragon or fennel, and thyme. Stir in white wine and strained fish stock. Simmer until flavours blend, to taste. Add salt and pepper, to taste.

Bring to boil over high heat. (If leaving lobster whole, add and return to boil). Add scallops, clams, mussels, fish and lobster pieces. Simmer for about 15 minutes or until all fish is cooked. Discard any unopened mussels. Taste, correct seasoning and add chopped parley or other garnish.

Makes generous meal for 2, which should be taken to table in cooking pot. Ladle broth and lobster into wide soup plates. Serve with crusty loaf of bread and butter or garlic toast.

Serves 2.

Fish Stock:
To 1½ qt/1.5 L water, add 1 to 2 lb/0.5 to 1 kg fish heads, bones and trimmings (lobster shells or bodies can also be added). Add large chopped onion, minced garlic clove, bayleaf, handful of parsley, a little thyme, and salt and pepper. Simmer, uncovered, about 1 hour. Strain.

An Old "Formula" Chowder

"Potatoes should be ⅓ done when onions go in, and onions all done when fish goes in. When everything begins to boil, chowder is done and should be eaten."

Salmon & Leek Bisque with Crème Fraîche

Crème fraîche is a French specialty — matured, thickened cream with a slightly tangy, nutty flavour and velvety rich texture.

2	shallots, minced	2
2	medium tomatoes, peeled, seeded and chopped	2
2	small leeks, chopped	2
4 tbsp	butter	60 mL
Pinch	tarragon	Pinch
1 tbsp	flour	15 mL
4 cups	fish or chicken stock (hot)	1 L
1 lb	salmon, poached and flaked*	500 g
½ cup	cream	125 mL
	Salt and pepper, to taste	
Dollop	Crème Fraîche (recipe follows) or sour cream	Dollop

* Canned salmon can be used — just remove skin and bone.

Sauté shallots, tomatoes and leeks in butter. Cook until leeks are nicely softened. Add tarragon, to taste. Blend in flour. Cook briefly. Stir in stock. Simmer gently 20 minutes. Add salmon and heat through. Purée until smooth using food processor or blender. Return to pot and whisk in cream. Heat through (do not boil). Season with salt and pepper, to taste. Garnish with dollop of crème fraîche or sour cream.

Serves 6.

Crème Fraîche:
Ideal in soups and sauces, as it can be boiled without curdling.

1 cup	whipping cream	250 mL
2 tbsp	buttermilk	30 mL

Combine ingredients in glass container. Cover and let stand at room temperature 8 to 24 hours, or until very thick. Stir well before covering and refrigerate up to 10 days.

Makes 1 cup/250 mL.

Oyster Chowder

This yummy chowder is suitable for serving to even the most important guest, and is certainly a treat for those special days at home when you just want to pamper yourself. It is reminiscent of a chowder created by Chef William Medynski and served at *The Five Fishermen* in Halifax.

24	shucked oysters, with liquor *or* 1 can (5 oz/142 g) oysters	24
½ cup	onion	125 mL
¼ cup	celery, chopped	60 mL
¼ cup	butter	60 mL
1½ cups	potatoes, diced	375 mL
½ cup	carrots, thinly sliced	125 mL
1½ cups	water	375 mL
1 tbsp	flour	15 mL
1 tsp	salt	5 mL
Dash	pepper	Dash
2 cups	milk	500 mL
1 tbsp	parsley, chopped	15 mL

Poach oysters in their liquor 4 to 5 minutes, or until edges begin to curl. Drain oysters, reserving juice; set aside.

Sauté onion and celery in butter. Add potatoes, carrots and water. Simmer slowly until vegetables are tender. Add flour, salt and pepper. Stir in milk and oyster juice. Cook until smooth. Add oysters and parsley. Reheat.

Serves 2 to 4.

California Avocado Clam Chowder

In the course of any conversation on the sacred rules of making clam chowder, most cooks concede that clams can be wedded to any number of different herbs and flavours as long as the fine flavour of the clam is not disturbed. This recipe is nothing like the recipes for traditional clam chowder — avocado gives it a gentle smoothness that enhances the taste of the clams. It is great served with hearts of romaine lettuce leaves, tossed lightly in lemon and oil, and a basketful of assorted crackers and toasted rolls.

2	onions (about 2 cups/500 mL), coarsely chopped	2
3	potatoes (about 1¼ lb/625 g), peeled and sliced	3
2	carrots, peeled and sliced	2
6	sprigs fresh parsley *or* 1 tbsp/15 mL dried parsley flakes	6
2	chicken bouillon cubes	2
1	bay leaf	1
½ tsp	thyme	2 mL
⅛ tsp	black pepper	0.5 mL
3	cans (6½ oz/175 mL each) minced or baby clams, drained and juice reserved	3
2½ cups	water	625 mL
1	large avocado (or 2 small — enough to equal 1¼ cups/310 mL), puréed*	1 or 2
½ cup	dry white wine	125 mL
2 tbsp	heavy cream	30 mL

* To prepare avocados, cut lengthwise around pit. Rotate halves in opposite directions to separate. One half will always keep pit. To remove pit, either slide tip of spoon gently underneath and lift out or carefully whack pit with sharp knife, embedding knife in pit. Rotate knife to lift pit out.

In large saucepan, combine first 8 ingredients with 2 cups/500 mL water and reserved juice from clams. Bring to boil; cover and simmer 15 minutes or until vegetables are barely tender. Add 1 can clams; simmer 5 minutes longer. Cool slightly. Remove bay leaf.

Purée vegetable-clam mixture in food processor or blender, adding small amounts at a time if necessary. Return purée to saucepan. Add remaining clams and ½ cup/125 mL water; combine and bring to boil. Simmer 5 minutes.

Meanwhile, seed, peel and purée avocado in food processor or blender. Combine avocado with wine and cream; whisk into soup purée over low heat. Serve immediately.

Serves 6 to 8.

Easy Shark Stew

Although we have called for shark in this recipe, any firm-fleshed fish will do. The joy of this one is that you can start with frozen fish and still have a quick delicious meal in half an hour. If you want to be super-organized, cut fresh fish into chunks before freezing.

2 lb	thresher shark, skin removed and cut into chunks	1 kg
1	can (14 oz/400 mL) chicken broth	1
2	cans (10 oz/284 mL each) French onion soup	2
1	can (8 oz/226 g) water chestnuts, sliced and drained	1
2	cans (14 oz/398 g each) Mexican-style stewed tomatoes	2
1	large onion, sliced	1
3	medium zucchini, sliced	3
	Salt and pepper, to taste	
	Garlic powder, to taste	

Place all ingredients in large stockpot. Bring to boil; reduce heat and simmer until fish is cooked, about 30 minutes.

Serves 4 to 6.

Norwegian Sea Chowder

I don't know where this recipe came from, but it's been in my personal recipe book for a long time. My notes indicate that I was attracted to it because of the unusual use of cloves and the slivered carrot and leek garnish. The soup is call "Palesuppe" and is sustaining enough to make a meal.

1½-2 lb	firm white fish (haddock, cod, monkfish)	0.75-1 kg
1	carrot, sliced	1
1	celery stalk, chopped	1
1	onion, chopped	1
4	peppercorns	4
2	cloves	2
1 tsp	salt	5 mL
1	bay leaf	1
	Water, to cover	
2 tbsp	butter	30 mL
3 tbsp	flour	45 mL
2 cups	milk	500 mL
½ cup	carrot, slivered	125 mL
½ cup	leek, slivered	125 mL
¼ cup	sour cream	60 mL
	Fresh herbs, chopped, as garnish	

Place fish along with sliced and chopped vegetables and seasonings in pot with enough water to cover. Bring to boil; lower heat and cook about 15 minutes, until fish flakes. Lift fish into bowl, flake and remove any bones or skin. Strain cooking liquid, reserving 2 cups/500 mL.

Melt butter in soup kettle or large saucepan. Stir in flour and cook over medium heat for 1 minute, stirring often. Slowly blend in reserved cooking liquid and milk. Bring to boil. Stir in slivers of fresh vegetables; simmer 4 to 5 minutes then lift out with slotted spoon. Return fish to pot, blend in sour cream and adjust seasonings.

Serve steaming hot in deep, warm bowls garnished with carrot and leek slivers and sprinkling of fresh herbs.

Serves 4 as a complete meal.

Lobster Corn Chowder

For a truly satisfying fireside supper, serve with chowder crackers, special breads, fresh fruit salad and chilled champagne. If you prefer a stovetop chowder rather than this microwave version, prepare according to your own recipe and add cooked lobster meat, heating through before serving.

2 tbsp	butter	30 mL
1 tbsp	flour	15 mL
1 tbsp	paprika	15 mL
1	8-oz/250-g potato, diced	1
½ cup	water	125 mL
1	celery stalk, minced	1
¼ cup	green pepper, minced	60 mL
¼ cup	onion, minced	60 mL
1 tsp	salt (optional)	5 mL
1	chicken-flavoured bouillon cube	1
1 pt	half-and-half	500 mL
1	pkg (10 oz/284 g) frozen whole kernel corn	1
1	can (11.3 oz/320 g) frozen lobster meat, thawed and drained well *or* 2½ cups/625 mL cooked lobster meat, removed from shell	1

In 3 qt/3 L casserole, melt butter in microwave on high; stir in flour and paprika. Add potato and next 6 ingredients. Cook, covered, on high for 10 to 12 minutes, until vegetables are tender, stirring twice during cooking. Add half-and-half and frozen corn. Cook 6 minutes.

While cooking, check lobster, removing any pieces shell or cartilage from claws. Slice tails and large claws into bite-size pieces, reserving 2 claws for garnish. Add lobster meat to chowder; stir in lobster and cook on high for 2 minutes or until heated through. Do not allow chowder to boil. Check that corn is tender before serving.

Serves 6 to 8.

Newfoundland Creamy Crab Soup

A woman from Newfoundland once told me that she never kept sherry in the house because they couldn't afford such luxury. The only liquor was that which came from someone's shed. She did, however, indulge in extracts when the "Watkins man came round." I find that "extracts" work quite well in recipes such as this one.

8 oz	crab meat, thawed if frozen	250 g
½ cup	onion, chopped	125 mL
½ cup	celery, chopped	125 mL
2 tbsp	butter	30 mL
2 tbsp	flour	30 mL
Dash	cayenne pepper	Dash
½ tsp	salt	2 mL
2 cups	milk	500 mL
1 cup	whipping cream	250 mL
1 tbsp	pale dry sherry	15 mL
1 tsp	lemon juice	5 mL
	Fresh herbs, for garnish (optional)	

Drain crab and remove bits of shell or cartilage. Chop larger pieces of meat.

Sauté onion and celery in butter until translucent, then blend in flour and seasonings. Stir to blend well, then add milk; stir and cook until sauce is smooth and thick.

Purée soup in blender. Return to pan. Add crab and cream and stir until heated through. Remove from heat and stir in sherry and lemon juice. Sprinkle with parsley or other herbs to garnish.

Serves 6.

Double Cheese & Clam Chowder

ACheddar and Swiss duet accents a creamy chowder brimming with clams. This is a rich chowder, so serve it as an appetizer in small (about 1 cup/250 mL) bowls, or make a meal of it with salad and rolls. You can use the juice drained off the clams to make your clam stock.

2	slices bacon, diced	2
4 tbsp	butter	60 mL
¼ cup	Spanish onion, finely chopped and firmly packed	60 mL
½ cup	celery, coarsely chopped	125 mL
½ cup	carrot, coarsely chopped	125 mL
4 tbsp	all purpose flour	60 mL
3⅔ cups	clam stock*, heated	920 mL
1 cup	potatoes, diced	250 mL
1	can (5 oz/142 g) baby clams, drained	1
¼ cup	35% cream	60 mL
½ cup	Cheddar cheese (medium), grated	125 mL
⅓ cup	Swiss cheese, grated	80 mL

* Make your own, use bottled clam juice, or substitute fish stock.

Sauté bacon in butter until golden brown. Add onions, celery and carrots; stir and cook until onions are transparent; do not brown.

Strain fat into large pot. Set vegetables aside. Heat fat; stir in flour until well blended. Gradually add heated clam stock, stirring constantly until mixture thickens. Stir in diced potatoes and reserved vegetables. Simmer until potatoes are tender; add clams and cream. Stir in grated cheeses; continue stirring over medium heat until blended. Serve immediately.

Serves 6.

Portuguese Creamy Mussel Dill Soup

This soup is not one we would habitually eat today because of the egg yolks and cream. I put it into the "sinful decadence" category and prepare it on those days when we say "hang the diets" — obviously, special occasions.

1½ cups	onion, chopped	375 mL
3 tbsp	butter or margarine	45 mL
3 tbsp	olive oil	45 mL
6 lb	mussels, cleaned	3 kg
1½ cups	dry white wine	375 mL
2 tbsp	fresh dillweed, snipped	30 mL
2 tbsp	parsley, minced	30 mL
	Salt and pepper, to taste	
4	egg yolks	4
1 cup	heavy cream	250 mL

In saucepan or soup kettle, sauté onion in butter and olive oil over medium-high heat until softened, about 5 minutes. Add wine and mussels; cover and bring to boil, steaming mussels until open, about 5 minutes.

Remove mussel meats from shells, reserving liquid — set aside 24 for garnish and remove black rims. Purée mussels and reserved liquor in food processor bitted with steel blade, or in blender.

Put purée in saucepan with dill, parsley, and salt and pepper to taste. Heat to boiling point, stirring often. Beat egg yolks and cream together, whisking a little soup into mixture. Add mixture to soup, whisking all the time. Heat and stir until soup is hot, but do not allow to boil.

Serve soup in heated bowls, garnished with reserved mussels and sprig of dill.

Serves 6.

Shrimp Gazpacho

Minced shrimp add an interesting texture to a basic gazpacho. Keep a few shrimp in reserve for a garnish.

1	slice dry white bread, crusts removed	1
¼ cup	fruity olive oil	60 mL
1 tsp	salt	5 mL
2	cloves garlic, minced	2
1 tbsp	wine vinegar	15 mL
1	English cucumber, peeled, halved and seeded*	1
3 cups	canned tomatoes plus juice	750 mL
1 lb	cooked shrimp, peeled and finely chopped	500 g
	Fresh basil	
	Pepper, to taste	
Dash	sour cream	Dash
	Croutons	

* Because size of cucumbers can vary so much, we suggest beginning by adding half, then checking consistency and taste and adding more if desired. If cucumber is small or medium size, we usually use the whole thing.

Soak bread in oil, salt and garlic for 1 hour. Combine with wine vinegar, half cucumber, and tomatoes. Purée until coarsely chopped. Add shrimp, basil and pepper. Chill well.

To serve, garnish with swirl of sour cream, croutons and reserved shrimp. If reserved shrimp are large, they will sink, so hook shrimp over rim of serving dish or slice in half lengthwise.

Serves 6.

Fish with Rouille

This soup is wonderful to have the day after a good old-fashioned lobster feed. Many people don't favour the body of the lobster, so you can just set them aside to use in this soup. I always try to save a little of the meat of the lobster as well, to add at the last minute — it really dresses up the soup. I freeze fish trimmings, leftovers and shells to make stock or use when I have enough for this kind of recipe. Serving it with rouille and cheese brings a new experience to your table. You should familiarize yourself with this recipe before starting to cook.

1	large onion, chopped	1
2	leeks, or another onion, chopped	2
½ cup	olive oil	125 mL
4	cloves garlic, mashed	4
1 lb	ripe tomatoes, roughly chopped *or* small can tomatoes, drained *or* 3 tbsp/45 mL tomato paste	500g
7 cups	water	1.75 L
2-3	sprigs parsley	2-3
1	bay leaf	1
½ tsp	thyme or basil	2 mL
2	large pinches fennel	2
2	large pinches saffron	2
1	2-inch/5-cm piece orange peel	1
2	large pinches pepper	2
1	whole medium potato, peeled	1
1 tbsp	salt	15 mL
3 lb	combined lean fish, fish heads, bones and trimmings	1.5 kg
2-3	lobster bodies and shells	2-3
2 oz	spaghetti or vermicelli, broken into pieces	60 g
6-8	thick slices French bread, hard-toasted (in oven)	6-8
	Swiss or Parmesan cheese, grated	
	Rouille (recipe follows)	

Cook onion and leeks slowly in olive oil for 5 minutes or until almost tender but not browned. Stir in garlic and tomatoes. Raise heat slightly and cook another 5 minutes. Add water, next 9 ingredients and fish (reserve half of lean fillets). Cook uncovered, at moderate boil, 30 to 40 minutes. Remove potato after 20 to 25 minutes when cooked through, and reserve for rouille.

Strain soup into second saucepan, pressing all juices out of ingredients. Stir in pasta and reserved fish cut into chunks, and cook at low boil for 10 to 12 minutes. If you have any reserved cooked lobster meat, add it for last 2 minutes of cooking.

Place bread into soup tureen or individual bowls and spoon soup over. Serve with cheese and rouille, passed separately.

Serves 6 to 8.

Rouille:
Rouille is a French term which refers to a fiery sauce of hot chilies and garlic. It is served as a garnish with fish and fish stews such as bouillabaisse. Rouille means "rust" — the dish was probably named because of its rust colour. This is just one version of a rouille, and it is probably not as hot as many others!

1 oz	canned pimento	30 mL
1	small chili pepper, boiled until tender	1
	or 4-5 drops Tabasco sauce	
1	medium potato, cooked in soup	1
4	cloves garlic, mashed	4
1 tsp	basil, thyme or savory	5 mL
4-6 tbsp	olive oil	60-90 mL
	Salt and pepper, to taste	
2-3 tbsp	hot soup	30-60 mL

Pound first 5 ingredients in bowl or mortar for a few minutes, to make smooth, sticky paste. Then, drop by drop, pound or beat in olive oil. Season to taste with salt and pepper. Just before serving, beat in hot soup, drop by drop. Serve in sauce boat.

Seafood Ragout with Basil Rouille

This delicate, well-seasoned stew looks elegant, with its clean broth, and tastes good enough to make a perfect meal when served with biscuits and a sparkling wine. Try to get scallops with roe if you can. We keep bay scallop shells on hand to serve the rouille in, or use the shells of the mussels.

2	leeks, sliced across, white part only	2
2	carrots, sliced across	2
1	stick celery, sliced across	1
2	garlic cloves, sliced	2
2	pieces ginger root, the size of quarters, smashed	2
1	bay leaf	1
1 cup	dry white wine	250 mL
2	tomatoes, chopped	2
8	mussels	8
6	medium shrimp, in shells	6
2	scallops	2
	Basil Rouille (recipe follows)	

Make stock by placing 1 leek and 1 carrot along with next 6 ingredients in pot. Bring to boil, then reduce heat to simmer for 20 minutes. Return to boil, toss in mussels and cook until open. Remove with tongs and cool slightly; remove meat from shells. Turn heat down, add shrimp and poach gently until shrimp turn pink and curl. Remove and cool; shell and slice shrimp meat into rounds.

Strain stock, pressing vegetables lightly for maximum flavour. You should have nice clear stock. Place remaining leek and carrot in stock, simmer 1 minute, then add scallops. Continue to simmer until scallops are cooked, about 4 minutes. Add mussels and shrimp and heat through. Serve with rouille.

Serves 2.

Basil Rouille:

¼ cup	fresh basil leaves, finely chopped	60 mL
1	tomato, peeled, seeded and finely diced	1
Pinch	cayenne	Pinch
	Salt and pepper, to taste	

Combine, seasoning to taste.

Scallop Soup

This hearty meal in a bowl has lots of veggies, delicious scallops and the added benefit of being very low in fat and calories.

2	carrots, cut into thin strips	2
1	onion, sliced	1
2	stalks celery, cut into thin strips	2
1	clove garlic, minced	1
2 tbsp	vegetable oil or margarine	30 mL
2½ cups	chicken broth	625 mL
2	tomatoes, seeded and diced	2
1 cup	mushrooms, sliced	250 mL
½ lb	scallops	250 g
1 tsp	basil	5 mL
¼ tsp	pepper	1 mL
1 tbsp	lemon juice	15 mL

In large saucepan or soup kettle, sauté carrots, onion, celery and garlic in melted oil or margarine until tender. Add chicken broth, bring to boil and simmer 5 minutes. Add tomatoes and mushrooms, scallops and seasonings. Simmer 5 minutes more, or until scallops are tender.

Serves 6.

Treasures of the Sea Soup

I first learned the trick of using creamed corn as a soup enhancer at a weight-loss class. I'm still trying to lose weight, but never forgot this recipe, even in my "fat" times. I've added to it over the years and it has now become a meal in itself. Don't be afraid to vary the seafood. We keep frozen lobster in our freezer, so open the can and use half for this soup and half for another dish the next day. Frozen or canned crab meat also works very well.

2 cups	milk	500 mL
1 cup	half-and-half	250 mL
1	can (6½ oz/175 mL) baby clams	1
1	can (4½ oz/128 mL) shrimp (or buy frozen baby shrimp)	1
6-8 oz	cooked lobster or crab meat, drained well, cartilage removed, chopped *or* 6-8 oz/185-250 g firm-fleshed fish fillet, such as haddock, cubed	185-250 g
4	strips streaky bacon, chopped small	4
1	clove garlic, minced	1
1 cup	dry white wine	250 mL
	Salt, to taste	
2-3	grinds fresh black pepper	2-3
½ tsp	dried thyme *or* 1 tbsp/15 mL fresh thyme, chopped	2 mL
1 lb	red potatoes*, diced	500 g
1	can (16 oz/455 mL) creamed corn	1
1 cup	tiny broccoli florettes	250 mL
4	green onions, chopped	4
2 tbsp	parsley, chopped	30 mL

* Any kind of potato will do, but we prefer a firm one such as a red or a Binji.

Measure out milk and half-and-half and allow to stand on counter to warm. Drain liquid off clam and shrimps, reserving both.

In large soup pot, sauté bacon until crisp, then sauté garlic. Add reserved seafood liquor, wine, salt if desired, pepper and thyme. Bring to boil. Add potatoes, cover and simmer until potatoes are tender (15 to 20 minutes). Add corn, onion, broccoli and parsley. Add milk and half-and-half. Bring to boil, stirring constantly. Reduce heat and add seafood.

Cook until heated, and, if using fresh fish, until fish is cooked. Taste and season with further salt and pepper, if required. Serve. Eat leftovers up next day. If too thick, add a little milk when reheating.

Serves 4 to 6.

Snapper Stew

This recipe comes out of the celebrations of the Pacific Seafood Festival. If you can't get Pacific Snapper, substitute any firm-fleshed white fish.

1	small onion, chopped	1
1	small zucchini, sliced	1
1	stalk celery, chopped	1
3 tbsp	olive oil	45 mL
4	medium-size ripe tomatoes, peeled and chopped	4
½ cup	fish or chicken stock	125 mL
1 tsp	sugar	5 mL
½ tsp	rosemary	2 mL
1	clove garlic, crushed	1
3 tbsp	flour	45 mL
3 tbsp	water	45 mL
1 lb	snapper fillets, cut into 1 inch/2.5 cm cubes	500 g

In large saucepan over medium heat, cook onion, zucchini, and celery in olive oil until tender-crisp. Add tomatoes, stock, sugar, rosemary and garlic. Bring to boil; cover and simmer 10 minutes.

Mix flour and water and add to contents of saucepan. Cook, stirring constantly, until sauce bubbles and thickens. Add snapper and cook over low heat until flesh is opaque and begins to open into flakes. Serve immediately with rice, pasta or potatoes.

Serves 4.

Butternut Squash Soup with Atlantic Lobster

The original recipe for this soup came from David Watt of *The Pineapple Inn Bakehouse* in Unionville, Ontario. The basil, old Cheddar and ale combine to give the soup a rich full flavour which marries well with the delicate taste and texture of lobster. Watt uses wild leeks and organic Cheddar, ale and chicken stock. We compromised and still managed to impress ourselves!

4 tbsp	unsalted butter	60 mL
2	onions, chopped	2
3	cloves garlic, chopped	3
3	leeks, chopped and thoroughly washed	3
2	medium-size butternut squash, peeled and roughly chopped	2
1	bottle ale	1
3 cups	chicken or vegetable stock	750 mL
Bunch	fresh basil (pick off 10 large leaves and tie remaining stems together with string)	Bunch
1	can (11.3 oz/320 g) frozen lobster meat, thawed and drained well *or* 2½ cups/625 mL cooked lobster meat, removed from shell	1
6 oz	Cheddar cheese, grated	185 g
	Salt and pepper, to taste	

Melt butter in saucepan over medium heat. Add onions, garlic, leeks and squash. Gently sauté 2 to 3 minutes. Add ½ ale and cover 5 minutes. Add stock and bring to boil; add basil stems. Simmer until squash is soft. Remove basil stems.

Purée squash mixture in blender or food processor. Add remaining ale, lobster and most of cheese. Season with salt and pepper, to taste. Thinly slice basil leaves and use them and remaining cheese to garnish soup. Serve.

Serves 4 to 6.

Oyster Artichoke Soup

Food snobs usually turn up their noses when they see a recipe that contains canned soup. I checked with some chefs who are friends and learned that they often use canned products as the base for a dish. The reason is twofold — the canned soup saves time and money and the product is consistently good. The secret is to find brands you prefer and build on them. When using canned soups, eliminate the salt until you can taste the final dish — some of the soups are highly salted.

½ cup	butter	125 mL
½ cup	green onion tops, chopped	125 mL
½ cup	mushrooms, sliced	125 mL
1 pt	oysters, shucked	500 mL
½ tsp	white pepper	2 mL
¼ tsp	salt	1 mL
Dash	red pepper	Dash
2	cans (10 oz/284 mL each) cream of celery soup	2
1	can artichoke hearts, packed in water, drained and coarsely chopped	1
1 pt	half-and-half	500 mL
⅛ cup	white wine	30 mL

Melt butter in heavy saucepan. Sauté onion tops and mushrooms. Add oysters, salt, and peppers. Heat until oysters begin to curl around edges. Add undiluted celery soup. Cook until smooth. Add artichokes. Cook until bubbling. Add half-and-half and allow to thicken. Add wine. Heat until very hot and serve.

Serves 8.

Pepper Pot Soup

This Jamaican-style soup dates back to the Arawak Indians, who prepared a stew that was kept going on the fire, and to which new ingredients were added every day.

1	pkg (10 oz/284 g) frozen okra, sliced	1
1 cup	fresh spinach, chopped	250 mL
1 cup	green bell pepper, seeded and chopped	250 mL
¼ cup	onion, minced	60 mL
½ tsp	salt	2 mL
½ tsp	thyme, crushed	2 mL
½ tsp	marjoram, crushed	2 mL
½ tsp	rosemary, crushed	2 mL
¼ tsp	garlic, minced	1 mL
Pinch	ground red pepper	Pinch
6 cups	chicken stock	1.5 L
2 lb	small shrimp (51-60 count), peeled and deveined	1 kg
1 cup	canned cream of coconut	250 mL
10	lime slices	10

Combine okra, spinach, green pepper, minced onion, salt, thyme, marjoram, rosemary, minced garlic, red pepper and chicken stock in large stockpot. Heat to boiling. Reduce heat; simmer, covered, 30 minutes. Add shrimp and coconut milk. Simmer until shrimp are cooked, about 5 minutes. Serve garnished with lime slices.

Serves 10.

Lobster Chowder

This rich chowder is reminiscent of those served in Atlantic Canada in days past, when cooks might use the water the lobster was cooked in instead of fish stock or clam juice. Today's tastes find that method a little too salty. The easiest and most economical way to make a lobster chowder is to use frozen broken meat, or body and leg meat. This is sold canned or vacuum packed and is not always readily available, so check out your local seafood store. Quite often, those who sell lobster will remove any meat at the end of the day and freeze it in tubs, or they may be willing to order in frozen products if asked. This chowder can be made ahead and stored in the refrigerator, covered, for up to 8 hours. Just reheat it slowly, without boiling. And be warned: this recipe falls into the sheer decadence category — don't think about those diets!

3 cups	water	750 mL
6 cups	potatoes, diced and peeled	1.5 kg
2	medium onions, diced	2
1	stalk tender celery, diced	1
1	can (11.3 oz/320 g) frozen lobster, thawed and drained	1
	or meat from 4 lobsters (about 1½ lb/750 g each)	
¼ cup	butter	60 mL
2 cups	light cream	500 mL
1 cup	heavy cream	250 mL
1½ cups	fish stock or bottled clam juice	375 mL
	Salt and pepper, to taste	

In large saucepan, bring water to boil; add potatoes, onions and celery; cook, covered, over medium-high to high heat, 5 to 10 minutes.

While potatoes are cooking, chop any large pieces of lobster and cook in 2 tbsp/30 mL of butter in medium-hot skillet, just until light golden. When potatoes are tender, add lobster, light and heavy cream, stock or juice, and remaining butter. Cook over medium heat for 3 to 5 minutes until heated through, being careful not to let mixture boil. Season with salt and pepper, to taste. Some cooks sprinkle a little parsley or paprika over each bowl as it is served.

Serves 12.

Fish Stock

M any recipes, particularly those for soups, stews and sauces, call for fish stock. You can buy an "instant" powder form, substitute bottled clam juice or make your own. We freeze fish stock in ice cube trays for future use. You can do the same thing with any broth left over after steaming mussels.

2 cups	dry white wine	500 mL
1	bay leaf	1
7-8	sprigs parsley and thyme, tied together	7-8
	Celery leaves, chopped	
1	onion, chopped	1
1	small carrot, diced	1
1	slice fresh ginger	1
1	green onion, chopped	1
1 lb	fish heads and backbones	500 g

Combine all ingredients and bring to boil. Lower heat and simmer gently 30 minutes. Strain and discard all but liquid. Refrigerate if using within next couple of days. To store for longer time, freeze in small portions.

Makes 2 cups/500 mL stock.

Mainly Delicious

Main Course Meals

The typical role of seafood is as the main course. Whether you are serving a one course meal, or a five course feast, seafood makes a lovely featured dish of choice.

Baked Lobster Omelette for Brunch

The brunch offers a casual way to entertain. The popular combined breakfast and lunch originated as a meal served after the hunt and has evolved to become one of the most popular entertaining occasions. The perfect entrée is Canadian lobster. It has built-in elegance and blends perfectly with breakfast ingredients to create unique omelettes that are quick and easy. Keep the menu simple and the occasion informal. Serve your favourite champagne or sparkling wine and complete the menu with warm muffins, stollen, brioche or biscuits, fruit butters, assorted cheeses and a variety of seasonal fruits and a special coffee. This recipe serves eight but is easy to expand to twelve by preparing half the omelette recipe again in an 8-inch square/2 L baking dish. Have the smaller omelette ready to go into the oven when you take out the first one and you will be able to offer piping hot "seconds" on the whistle. They will disappear in no time.

½ cup	flour	125 mL
1 tsp	baking powder	5 mL
12	eggs	12
5	drops Tabasco sauce	5
1 lb	lobster meat, cut into bite-size pieces (if using frozen lobster, thaw and drain well)	500 g
1 lb	Monterey Jack cheese, grated	500 g
2 cups	creamed cottage cheese	500 mL
½ cup	butter, melted	125 mL
	Salt and freshly ground pepper, to taste	

Preheat oven to 400°F/200°C and butter 9x13 inch/3.5 L baking dish. Sift flour with baking powder. Beat eggs and add Tabasco. Stir in flour, lobster, cheeses, butter; season with salt and pepper.

Pour mixture into baking dish and bake 15 minutes. Reduce heat to 350°F/180°C and bake 15 minutes longer or until omelette is puffed and light golden brown on top. Cut into 12 squares and serve at once.

Serves 8.

White Lobster Chili

This wonderful variation on an old dish comes from one of the most creative cooks I know — one of the few people I can call in the middle of the night to discuss food! She has a reputation for always doing something new, unique and unusual, and doing it with panache. This one dish supper or buffet will enhance your reputation while delighting guests with the taste and you with the ease of preparation.

2 cups	onions, coarsely chopped	500 mL
5	garlic cloves, minced	5
2 tbsp	vegetable oil	30 mL
2	jalapeño peppers, chopped	2
1	can (4 oz/125 g) mild green chilies, chopped	1
2 tbsp	lemon juice	30 mL
2 tsp	ground cumin	10 mL
1 tsp	oregano	5 mL
½ tsp	cayenne pepper	2 mL
½ tsp	salt	2 mL
2 cups	chicken stock	500 mL
1	can (14 oz/400 g) white (cannellini) or red kidney beans, drained and rinsed	1
1½ lb	lobster meat, cut into bite-size pieces	750 g
½ cup	fresh cilantro, coarsely chopped	125 mL

Optional Garnishes: grated Monterey Jack, Cheddar or Mozzarella cheese, chopped cilantro, crushed red pepper flakes or salsa

In large saucepan, over medium-high heat, sauté onions and garlic in oil until onion is tender (about 5 minutes). Add jalapeños, chilies, lemon juice, cumin, oregano, cayenne pepper and salt; cook 1 minute. Add chicken stock and beans and bring to boil. Reduce heat and simmer uncovered for 20 minutes or until slightly thickened.

Add lobster meat and cook another 10 minutes. Stir in cilantro. To serve, ladle into bowls and garnish with cheese, chopped cilantro, red pepper flakes or salsa.

Serves 8.

Rigatoni with Lobster
& Smoked Turkey

In this recipe, nutritious, delicious pasta partners succulent lobster. Rigatoni is used here, but ziti, penne or other pasta shapes work equally well.

2 tbsp	olive oil	30 mL
8 oz	rigatoni, ziti or penne pasta	250 g
4	cloves garlic, crushed	4
¼ cup	whites of green onion, chopped	60 mL
¼ cup	tomato, seeded, skinned and chopped	60 mL
2 tbsp	yellow pepper, finely chopped	30 mL
½ cup	dry white wine	125 mL
2 tbsp	fresh basil, chopped	30 mL
½ tsp	dried red pepper, crushed	2 mL
¾ cup	heavy cream or half-and-half	180 mL
	Salt and pepper (optional)	
1½ cups	cooked lobster meat, chopped	375 mL
6 oz	smoked turkey, diced into ½ inch/1 cm squares (smoked salmon can be substituted)	185 g
¼ cup	Parmesan cheese, freshly grated	60 mL

Bring large pot of salted water and 1 tbsp/15 mL olive oil to boil. Add pasta and cook 8 minutes, or until *al dente*. Drain and rinse under running water. Drain again.

Heat 1 tbsp/15 mL oil in heavy saucepan over medium-high heat. Add garlic and onion; sauté 2 minutes. Add tomato, yellow pepper and wine. Cook for additional 2 minutes; add basil, red pepper and cream. Continue cooking until liquid is reduced by half (about 5 minutes). Taste and season with salt and/or pepper, if desired.

Add lobster, turkey and pasta and gently sauté until heated, 1½ to 2 minutes. Place on serving platter or 4 individual plates; top with Parmesan. If using fresh Parmesan, top dish under preheated broiler for about 30 seconds to brown cheese. Serve immediately.

Serves 4.

Note: If buying 11.3 oz/320 g can frozen lobster meat, use larger portions in this pasta dish and save smaller broken meat for a delicious sandwich filling. For a classic presentation, slice tail meat into medallions and use claws for garnish.

Lobster & Scallops in Champagne Sauce

Requiring a half-bottle of Champagne, this makes an elegant dish for a special occasion. If you prefer, you can substitute Gewurtztraminer or another sparkling wine for the Champagne.

1 lb	lobster meat (reserve juices)	500 g
2 cups	Brut Champagne	500 mL
4 tbsp	butter	60 mL
2	medium carrots, cut into long, thin strips	2
1	leek (white portion and a little of the green), trimmed, halved lengthwise, rinsed well and cut into long, thin strips	1
1	celery stalk, cut into quarters and then into long, thin strips	1
2 tbsp	flour	30 mL
1 cup	clam nectar*	250 mL
1 cup	whipping cream	250 mL
½ lb	scallops	250 g
1	lemon, juice of	1
	Salt and freshly ground pepper, to taste	
Dash	nutmeg	Dash

* Bottled clam juice is available in the specialty section of grocery stores.

Combine lobster juice and Champagne in saucepan. Over medium-high heat, reduce liquid to 1 cup/250 mL. Strain stock and set aside.

In large skillet over medium heat, melt butter and sauté vegetables until crisp-tender. Taste, and season with salt and pepper. Add flour to vegetables and cook for about 1 minute, stirring constantly. Add stock, clam nectar and whipping cream; cook for about 1 minute or until just done. Add lemon juice, salt, pepper and nutmeg. Serve.

Serves 4 to 6.

Chef William's Fishermen Scallops

I cut this recipe from a newspaper in 1984 and it remains a favourite. The creator is Chef William Medynski of *The Five Fishermen* restaurant in Halifax. It is rich and expensive, a dish to serve on a very special occasion to very special people. It's also a great make-ahead meal for those lucky guests.

½ cup	butter	125 mL
1 tsp	curry powder	5 mL
1	whole shallot, diced	1
1½ cups	flour	375 mL
2½ oz	white wine	75 mL
½ tsp	tarragon	2 mL
¼ tsp	white pepper	1 mL
1 tsp	lime juice	5 mL
1 qt	sour cream	1 L
3½ lb	scallops	1.75 kg
¼ cup	water	60 mL
1 oz	chicken soup base	30 mL
3	strands saffron*	3

* The saffron is expensive but important to the recipe, not only for colour but also for the flavour it imparts.

Combine last 3 ingredients and heat separately.

Melt butter in large saucepan. Add curry powder and shallot. Cook 5 minutes over low heat. Stir in flour and cook 5 minutes more. Add wine and mix well, allowing mixture to thicken. Stir in combination of water, chicken base and saffron. Add tarragon and pepper. Add sour cream in ½ qt/0.5 L quantities, heating between each addition. Strain and cool.

Place scallops in casserole dish; pour sauce over top and marinate 24 hours before serving. Bake in 500°F/260°C oven 10 to 12 minutes. A nice addition to this recipe is to top casserole with grated Brick cheese before baking.

Serves 8.

Scallop Collage

The chef who gave me this recipe is a whiz at making puff pastry. However, I confess to buying mine from a local bakery. You can also purchase it frozen.

4½ oz	mushrooms, minced	140 g
4 oz	onion, minced	125 g
4 tbsp	butter	60 mL
1 lb	puff pastry dough	500 g
16	large scallops	16
1	egg yolk, beaten	1
	Fish Velouté (recipe follows)	

Sauté mushrooms and onions lightly in butter. Drain well, until mixture is firm and dry.

Roll out pastry dough until about ¼ inch/0.5 cm thick. Cut into 8 3-inch/7-cm squares. Divide onion and mushroom mixture among squares. Top each with 2 scallops. Dab corners of pastry with egg yolk, then draw corners together and pinch closed so that each creates small sealed sachet. Place on baking sheet and bake at 450°F/230°C for 10 minutes, or until golden brown.

While baking, prepare Velouté. To serve, spoon Velouté onto plate, then arrange sachets in Velouté and garnish with fresh herbs.

Serves 4.

Fish Velouté:

½ cup	butter	125 mL
⅔ cup	flour, sifted	160 mL
12½ oz	fish stock	390 mL
1 oz	brandy	30 mL

Melt butter in sauté pan until clear. Add sifted flour slowly, stirring constantly until tan colour is reached and mixture is smooth. Keep on low heat. Add fish stock slowly, stirring constantly until sauce is of uniform consistency. Add brandy; keep over low heat and reduce sauce by ¼. Serve immediately.

Spaghetti Squash with Seafood

Each Fall we eagerly anticipate the arrival of fresh spaghetti squash, which we enjoy for its crunch and nutty flavour. Because we enjoy it so much we use it as a substitute for spaghetti, or as a main course in dishes like this one. Split the spaghetti squash in half lengthwise, remove seeds, turn upside down in a glass pie plate, add ½ cup/125 mL of water, cover with plastic wrap and microwave six to nine minutes, depending on size. You can also bake spaghetti squash in the oven — use a fork to loosen the spaghetti-like strands and they're ready to serve. We prefer not to overcook them, so that they have a slight crunch.

½ cup	onions, chopped	125 mL
1	clove garlic, minced	1
1 tbsp	margarine, melted	15 mL
1 tbsp	olive oil	15 mL
3 cups	tomatoes, peeled and seeded	750 mL
1 tbsp	tomato paste	15 mL
¼ tsp	dried oregano	1 mL
2 cups	seafood such as lobster meat, small shrimp, tuna, crab, mussels, clams or oysters	500 g
	Salt and pepper, to taste	
1 large or 2 small	spaghetti squash, cooked and flesh removed	1 or 2

Sauté onions and garlic in margarine and oil. Add tomatoes, tomato paste and oregano. Simmer, stirring often, for 20 minutes. Add seafood. Add salt and pepper to taste, and simmer 5 to 7 minutes or until seafood is cooked. Serve over hot spaghetti squash.

Serves 2 to 4.

Microwaved Creole Stuffed Spuds

A big baked potato, hot and fluffy, is a super base for a tangy sauce. Even large potatoes contain only 175 calories and can be built into a quick and easy meal by using your microwave. In Louisiana, these spuds would be made with crawfish, crab meat or shrimp.

4	large baking potatoes (8 oz/250 g each), scrubbed	4
1 tbsp	butter or margarine	15 mL
2 tbsp	celery, chopped	30 mL
2 tbsp	red, orange or yellow bell pepper, chopped	30 mL
1 tbsp	green onion, sliced	15 mL
½ lb	small shrimp (or use solid tuna broken into bite-size chunks)	250g
1	can (8 oz/226 g) tomato sauce	1
½ tsp	sugar	2 mL
⅛ tsp	pepper	0.5 mL
⅛ tsp	ground red pepper	0.5 mL
Dash	Tabasco sauce (optional)	Dash

Prick potatoes several times with fork. Arrange on microwave-safe paper towels, leaving at least 1 inch/2.5 cm between spuds. Microwave on high, 14 to 17 minutes or until done. Turn at least once during cooking.

Using microwave-safe, uncovered bowl, microwave butter, celery, pepper and onion on high, 2 to 3 minutes. Vegetables should be tender. Stir in shrimp or tuna, tomato sauce, sugar, pepper, red pepper and Tabasco. Cook uncovered on high 3 to 5 minutes to heat through.

Place potatoes on serving plates after gently rolling each between folds of towel or 2 hot pads (to fluff up flesh). Cut "X" into top of each and push in ends to open up potato. Divide sauce between potatoes and enjoy.

Serves 4.

Note: In low wattage ovens, you may have to extend cooking time.

Red Snapper Excellence

What I like about the method of cooking in this recipe is that I can finish off my table and the vegetable dishes while the fish bakes. Try substituting other fish for red snapper, if you like.

3 tbsp	lemon juice	45 mL
1 tbsp	white-wine Worcestershire sauce*	15 mL
¼ tsp	salt (optional)	1 mL
	Black pepper, freshly ground, to taste	
4	red snapper fillets, of equal size (about 4 oz/125 g each)	4
¼ cup	butter or margarine	60 mL
⅓ cup	all purpose flour	80 mL
1	large egg, beaten with 1 tbsp/15 mL water	1
2 tsp	cilantro	10 mL

* If you don't have the white-wine type, use regular Worcestershire Sauce.

Combine lemon juice, Worcestershire sauce, salt, pepper and cilantro in shallow dish. Add fillets, turning to thoroughly coat. Cover and refrigerate at least 2 hours, or overnight.

Heat oven to 350°F/180°C. Drain fish. Melt butter in large ovenproof skillet, over medium heat. Coat fish with flour, shaking off excess. Dip into egg mixture, coating all sides. Place skin side up in skillet and cook 3 minutes, turning once.

Remove from element and place in oven; bake 10 minutes, or until fish is opaque in centre at thickest point.

Serves 4.

White Mountain Trout with Maple Dijon Vinaigrette

It is ironic that the first time I had trout cooked and served by a cowboy squatting by a fire, I was at Ignatius College, a religious farm community in Guelph, Ontario. The event was "Feast of the Fields," one of the best eating experiences one can imagine. It happens every fall in Ontario. This recipe from Matthew Jamieson of the *Sierra Grill* restaurant in Barrie, Ontario was wonderful. He adapted it from an old Vermont recipe dating back to the 1880s, and advocates using organic trout. Any trout, however, will do.

Organic trout fillets (deboned)
Cornmeal seasoned with salt and pepper
Bacon drippings for frying
Maple Dijon Vinaigrette (see recipe below)

Prepare trout fillets by checking for bones and removing any you find. Leave skin on. Pat dry and dredge in cornmeal. Fry in hot skillet with bacon drippings. Serve with spoonful of vinaigrette over fish.

Maple Dijon Vinaigrette:

3 tbsp	Dijon mustard	45 mL
1 cup	olive oil	250 mL
½ cup	maple syrup	125 mL
4 tbsp	balsamic vinegar	60 mL
1 tsp	ground ginger	5 mL
1 tsp	salt and pepper	5 mL
1 tsp	ground thyme	5 mL
1 tsp	dried oregano	5 mL
	Juice of 1 lemon	

Emulsify together Dijon mustard and olive oil. Add remaining ingredients and mix thoroughly. Let sit for 1 hour and serve over fish. Sauce may be made ahead and keeps well.

Makes approximately 2 cups/500 mL.

Saffron Seafood Cream

This showy dish deserves to be the focal point of any dinner party. Serve over puff pastry shells which have been prebaked, or over white, long grain rice which has been gently tossed with butter and chopped fresh cilantro or parsley leaves. Garnish with leaves from the fennel or cilantro. It's an eye-catching meal, especially when served in a copper chafing dish.

2	large fennel bulbs, cut into small wedges	2
2	medium-size carrots, cut into matchsticks	2
1	small red pepper, cut into matchsticks	1
1	small yellow pepper, cut into matchsticks	1
½ lb	button mushrooms	250 g
1 lb	large sea scallops	500 g
½ lb	jumbo shrimp, shelled and deveined	250 g
16	large cultured mussels	16
1	can (11.3 oz/320 g) frozen lobster meat*, thawed and drained *or* meat from 2 1½ lb/750 g lobsters	1
3 tbsp	butter or margarine	45 mL
3 tbsp	extra virgin olive oil	45 mL
½ tsp	anise seeds, crushed	2 mL
1 qt	half-and-half	1 L
½ tsp	saffron threads, crushed	2 mL
½ cup	seafood stock (from cooking lobster or mussels, or use bottled clam juice)	125 mL

* Be sure to buy a can of lobster meat that contains claws and tails, rather than broken meat.

Assemble vegetables. Check seafood. There should be no broken shells in scallops, shrimp should be deveined, mussels should be clean and have beards removed, lobster should be well drained.

Place mussels in saucepan with ¼ cup/50 mL water. Bring to boil, reduce heat and steam, covered, until shells open, about 5 minutes. Discard any mussels that do not open. Heat 2 tbsp each butter and oil in 8 qt/8 L Dutch oven. Add vegetables and anise and cook over medium-high heat, until tender, stirring frequently. Remove vegetables, being sure to drain any cooking liquid back into pan. Add remaining butter and olive oil and cook shrimp until tender. Remove, and cook scallops until opaque and tender when tested with fork. Remove.

Stir stock into butter remaining in Dutch Oven. Heat to boiling, while scraping to free delicious browned morsels left in pan. Cook 5 minutes. Add half-and-half and saffron. Over high heat, heat to boiling; boil 5 minutes. Add seafood and vegetables. Taste sauce and, if desired, add small amount of salt. Heat through. Serve in chafing dish, or serving dish that will keep mixture warm, over puff pastry or rice.

Serves 8.

Scallops Balsamic

This dish is so quick and easy to prepare it could almost be considered fast food. Have everything ready before starting to cook — these scallops should be eaten hot. Balsamic vinegar has been made from the juice of sweet trebiano grapes for 800 years in the Modena region of Italy. In a carefully controlled fermentation process, the juice is moved through a succession of large wooden barrels made of chestnut, ash, locus, mulberry, oak and juniper, for an aging that may take as long as 50 years. The final product is a rich dark-coloured liquid with an earthy, yet mellow, taste.

2 tbsp	unsalted butter	30 mL
1	shallot, minced	1
1	clove garlic, minced	1
12 oz	bay scallops	375 g
1½ tbsp	basil, finely chopped	20 mL
1 tbsp	balsamic vinegar	15 mL
	Salt and freshly ground pepper, to taste	

Sauté shallot and garlic in butter over high heat, stirring frequently until softened, about 2 minutes. Add scallops and basil; cook, stirring frequently 2 minutes. Add vinegar and cook further 2 to 3 minutes, until heated through. Season with salt, if desired, and pepper. Serve immediately.

Serves 2 to 3.

Salmon with Beurre Blanc

T his elegant French-style creation is superb for any dinner party.

1	small onion, cut in half	1
6	whole cloves	6
2	small carrots, peeled	2
¾ cup	dry white wine	180 mL
¾ cup	water	180 mL
1	head parsley	1
1	branch rosemary	1
1-2	sprigs thyme	1-2
Pinch	salt	Pinch
1	whole salmon (6-8 lb/3-4 kg)	1
	Fresh basil	
	Beurre Blanc (recipe follows)	

In fish poacher place onion studded with cloves, carrots, wine, water, parsley, rosemary, thyme and sprinkle of salt. Bring to boil, cover and simmer 10 minutes. Allow to cool. Place fish on tray in poacher and cook, covered, over simmering wine mixture 20 minutes, or until fish is done.

Remove fish to heat-safe platter, carefully removing skin. Take whole fish to table, with sauce on side, or carefully remove fillets from backbone to serve on individual plates. Place fish in warm oven while making Beurre Blanc with reserved poaching liquid. To serve, garnish fish with basil leaves.

Serves 8.

Beurre Blanc:

2	shallots, chopped	2
½ cup	wine vinegar	125 mL
1	egg yolk	1
7-8 tbsp	butter	105-120 mL
¼ cup	poaching liquid, strained	60 mL
	Cornstarch, if needed	

Place shallots and vinegar in small saucepan and boil until reduced by ½. Remove most shallots and discard. Beat in egg yolk. With pan over low heat, whisk in butter a small amount at a time. (If it starts to separate, whisk in dash of cold water.) Add poaching liquid. If sauce is thin, sprinkle with 1-2 tsp/5-10 mL cornstarch, whisking vigorously to blend. Cook until slightly thickened.

Curried Shrimp

The garam masala used in this recipe is an Indian blend of as many as twelve spices which add a "warmth" to Indian food. It is usually added to a dish towards the end of cooking, or sprinkled over the surface just before serving. You can make your own or buy it in the spice department of grocery stores.

1 tbsp	vegetable oil	15 mL
1	large onion, finely chopped	1
2 tsp	curry powder	10 mL
2	bay leaves	2
1	can (14 oz/398 mL) coconut milk	1
½ tsp	garam masala	2 mL
¼ cup	fresh coriander, finely chopped	60 mL
2 tbsp	lime juice (about 1 lime)	30 mL
1½ lb	medium shrimp, peeled and deveined	750 g
	Salt, to taste	
	Cayenne pepper, to taste	

Heat oil in large frying pan over medium heat. Add onion and cook 5 minutes until soft, stirring frequently. Stir in curry powder and bay leaves. Add coconut milk, garam masala, coriander and lime juice. Add shrimp.

Bring to boil, then reduce heat and simmer 4 to 5 minutes, or until shrimp are cooked through — they should be pink. Season with salt and cayenne, to taste.

Serves 6.

Steamer Fillets with Vegetable Medley

It was my tightwad nature that led me to try steaming. It seemed wicked to waste all of the heat generated by pots cooking on the stovetop, so we purchased bamboo steamers and cooked potatoes or pasta in the pot, with various veggies in two or three steamers placed on top. It didn't take us long to discover that steamed food retained much more flavour and texture, and we were adding no fat or salt. We soon added fish to our repertoire. Today there are a variety of steamers on the market. We use a metal sieve dropped into a pot, or our old bamboo steamers, depending on the amount of food being cooked. Some cooks advise lining the strainer with foil to retain natural juices; we prefer to use more natural lettuce leaves.

For an especially pleasing presentation, cook two types of fillets, such as halibut and salmon, to serve together. The combination of white and orange fish is colourful and delightful.

2 tbsp	lemon juice	30 mL
1 tbsp	Dijon mustard	15 mL
2 tsp	vegetable oil	10 mL
½ tsp	pepper, coarsely ground	2 mL
2	cloves garlic, minced	2
1½ cups	yellow squash, sliced	375 mL
	Lettuce leaves	
2	4-oz/125-g salmon, haddock or halibut fillets (or 1 each) about ½ inch/1.5 m thick	2
1	medium leek (about ½ lb/250 g), cleaned and cut in about 6 inch/15 cm lengths	1
2	fresh broccoli spears	2
2	cauliflower florettes	2
6	snow peas	6
	Lemon wedges	

Combine lemon juice, mustard, oil, pepper and garlic, mixing well. Toss 1 tbsp/15 mL of mixture with squash and set aside. Spread remaining mixture over fish fillets; set aside.

Arrange lettuce leaves in steamer, then place leek halves on top. Place over boiling water, cover and steam 4 minutes. Add broccoli, cauliflower and snow peas; cover and steam 2 minutes. Arrange squash over broccoli, place fish over vegetables and steam additional 5 minutes. When fish flakes easily, it is cooked. Watch that your boiling water does not boil dry. Be careful not to break fillets when removing fish to warm serving plates. Serve with vegetables, discarding lettuce. Garnish with lemon wedges.

Serves 2.

Shrimp & Scallop Dijon

½ lb	large, fresh, raw shrimp, cleaned with shell removed	250 g
½ lb	fresh scallops	250 g
	Zest and juice of small lemon	
2 tbsp	Dijon mustard	30 mL
2 tbsp	honey	30 mL
2 tbsp	olive oil	30 mL
1	bunch green onions, sliced	1
8	large mushrooms, sliced	8
1-2 tsp	flour	5-10 mL
1 tbsp	cold water	15 mL
4 cups	rice, cooked and hot	1 L

Drain shrimp and place with scallops in bowl. Sprinkle lemon zest and juice over all. Stir in mustard and honey and mix well. Marinate in mixture 30 minutes.

Heat olive oil in wok. Add green onions and mushrooms and sauté over high heat until mushrooms are tender. Add seafood and marinade, cooking over high heat until fully cooked. Be careful not to overcook.

Mix flour and water until smooth and stir into liquid in bottom of wok. Continue to cook and stir until thickened. Serve immediately over bed of rice.

Serves 4.

Poached Trout in Milk

I grew up eating fish poached in milk, although ours was usually Finnan Haddie. This cooking method went out of favour until the concern about healthy eating swept North America. Use 1% milk for a very low-fat cooking method that retains flavour and moisture. The poaching liquid can form the basis for a sauce, or you can discard it and use another sauce or topping for your trout. Refer to the listing at the beginning of this book on how to eat whole fish for tips about the best presentation. Whether you leave the head and tail on is optional.

2	6-8 oz/185-250 g fresh pan-dressed trout (if using frozen, thaw*)	2
¾ cup	milk	180 mL
½ cup	water	125 mL
¼ cup	celery leaves	60 mL
1	small onion, sliced into rings	1
1	small carrot, cut in julienne strips	1
2	sprigs parsley	2
4	peppercorns	4
¾ tsp	dried dillweed	3 mL
½ tsp	salt	2 mL
⅛ tsp	pepper	0.5 mL
1½ tsp	cornstarch	7 mL
1 tbsp	cold water	15 mL
1 tbsp	dry sherry, or more to taste	15 mL
⅛ tsp	paprika	0.5 mL

* You can cook frozen fish by increasing cooking time 5 to 10 minutes. I prefer to let frozen fish stand at room temperature, or if vacuum packed or in a plastic bag, immerse in cold water to thaw.

Combine milk, water, celery leaves, onion, carrot, parsley, peppercorns, dillweed, salt and pepper in deep, large skillet. Heat to boiling, then reduce to simmer, covered, for 10 minutes to blend flavours. Place fish in broth; return to boil. Reduce heat, cover and simmer about 12 minutes, or until fish flakes easily when tested with fork. Remove fish, cover and keep warm until ready to serve.

Strain poaching liquid through fine sieve lined with coffee filter or cheesecloth. Put ½ cup/125 mL poaching liquid into small saucepan. If there is not enough liquid, top up with water. Stir in cornstarch combined with cold water and cook, stirring until thick and bubbly. Cook 2 minutes then remove from heat and stir in sherry and paprika.

Prepare fish for serving by removing skin and backbone. Serve with sauce.

Serves 2.

Lobster Etouffée

E touffée literally means "smothered"; in Louisiana cooking, it signifies "covered with a liquid." This recipe is adapted from one by Hazel White, one of the fine cooks on Avery Island where Tabasco sauce was invented in 1868 and continues to be produced today.

¼ cup	vegetable oil	60 mL
1 cup	onion, finely chopped	250 mL
½ cup	celery, finely chopped	125 mL
½ cup	green pepper, finely chopped	125 mL
2	cloves garlic, minced	2
1 tbsp	tomato paste	15 mL
1 tsp	cornstarch	5 mL
¾ cup	clam juice or seafood broth	180 mL
8	peeled shrimp (optional)	8
¼ cup	green onions, thinly sliced	60 mL
¼ cup	parsley, chopped	60 mL
½ tsp	Tabasco sauce	2 mL
¼ tsp	salt	1 mL
2 cups	lobster meat, with larger pieces chopped	500 mL
	or 1 can (11.3 oz/320 g) frozen lobster meat, thawed	
4 cups	rice, cooked and hot	1 L

In large skillet, heat oil over medium-high heat. Add onion, celery, green pepper and garlic; cook 8 to 10 minutes or until tender, stirring frequently. Stir in tomato paste; cook 1 minute.

In small bowl, stir together cornstarch and clam juice until smooth. Add to vegetables in skillet. Stirring constantly, bring to boil over medium heat. Add shrimp, green onions, parsley, Tabasco sauce and salt. Stirring frequently, cook 3 minutes. Add lobster and continue to stir until shrimp is pink and lobster just heated through. Do not overcook. Serve immediately over rice.

Serves 4.

Pasta with Red Clam Sauce

It is possible to vary the type of pastas used in this recipe. We prefer a wholewheat spagettini or rotini. Always use a heavy saucepan when cooking tomato-based sauces, for better heat distribution and to prevent scorching. I also try to use a deep pan to prevent messing up my stove!

1 tbsp	olive oil	15 mL
1	large onion, chopped	1
3	cloves garlic, minced	3
1	can (28 oz/796 mL) stewed tomatoes	1
3 tbsp	tomato paste	45 mL
1	can (5 oz/142 g) baby clams, drained, reserving juice	1
½ tsp	dried oregano	2 mL
Pinch	hot pepper flakes	Pinch
1 tsp	dried parsley	5 mL
	Salt and pepper, to taste	
¾ lb	rotini pasta, cooked	375 g
½ cup	Parmesan cheese, freshly grated	125 mL
2 lb	small fresh clams	1 kg

Put oil in saucepan and heat over medium heat. Add onion and garlic, stirring about 5 minutes or until softened. Add tomatoes (crushing with fork) and tomato paste. Add juice from clams, oregano and hot pepper flakes. Bring to boil and immediately reduce heat. Simmer for ½ hour or so.

Add canned clams, parsley, and salt and pepper to taste. After sauce cooks about 20 minutes, put ½ cup/125 mL water in second pan and bring to boil; add fresh clams, steaming until done. Serve pasta, top with sauce and rim plate with clams in shell. Sprinkle all with Parmesan.

Serves 4.

Clam & Corn Pie

This recipe dates back forty years or so. The original calls for fresh corn, but you can use canned or frozen — just reduce the cooking time of the corn.

2	medium potatoes, diced	2
¼ cup	onion, chopped	60 mL
2 cups	fresh corn	500 mL
3 tbsp	butter	45 mL
3 tbsp	flour	45 mL
1 cup	milk	250 mL
2	cans (6½ oz/184 g each) baby or minced clams drained, reserving ½ cup/125 mL of clam broth	2
2 tbsp	parsley, chopped	30 mL
	Salt and pepper, to taste	
	Pastry to top 10 inch/25 cm pie	

Boil potatoes and onions for 2 minutes in as little water as possible. Add fresh-off-the-cob corn and cook through or until potatoes are tender.

Melt butter in separate pan and stir in flour until bubbly. Remove from heat and add milk combined with ½ cup/125 mL drained clam broth. Return to heat, cook and stir until just below boiling. Stir vegetables and clams into milk mixture and season carefully. Pour into buttered 10 inch/25 cm pie plate and cover with rich pastry. Cut slits for steam to escape. Bake in hot oven at 400°F/200°C, for about 30 minutes.

Serves 4.

Smoked Fish Casserole

When I was a young girl, my mother used to cook smoked haddock, or Finnan Haddie, in milk. I still enjoy it that way today. It was in the Maritimes that I learned to put smoked fillets into a casserole.

3	medium potatoes	3
2 tbsp	flour	30 mL
2 tbsp	butter	30 mL
1 cup	milk	250 mL
1 lb	smoked fish fillets such as haddock, cubed	500 g
1 cup	onion rings, thinly sliced	250 mL
	Salt and pepper, to taste (optional)	
½ cup	cheese, grated (optional)	125 mL
¼ cup	toast crumbs	60 mL

Cook potatoes in skins for 20 minutes, or until partially cooked. Make white sauce in double boiler with flour, butter and milk. When potatoes are partially cooked, peel and slice. In 1½ qt/1.5 L greased casserole dish, place potatoes, fish and onions in layers, sprinkling each with salt and pepper, if desired. Begin and end with layer of potatoes. Carefully pour white sauce over top and sprinkle with toast crumbs and grated cheese. Bake in moderate oven 350°F/180°C for 45 minutes.

Serves 4 to 6.

Cowboy Style Pan-Fried Brook Trout

For a long time I had a dream of camping in the west, beside a bubbling stream in a lush valley rimmed with snowcapped mountains. During a visit to Wyoming I found the valley and a stream, but didn't get to fulfil the fantasy of cooking up freshly caught brook trout. Later, however, at the Buffalo Bill Cody Museum in Cody, Wyoming, I did meet a gentleman who gave me the secret to "doin' it up raght." This is his recipe. To get the true taste you need a cast-iron frypan, and, if possible, a campfire.

2 cups	flour	500 mL
½ tsp	salt	2 mL
1 tsp	pepper	5 mL
6	brook trout, cleaned, washed and wiped dry (remove heads and tails, if you wish)	6
½ lb	bacon	250 g

Mix flour, salt and pepper together. Roll trout in flour mixture and set aside. Cook up bacon in hot skillet. When done, set aside.

Roll trout in flour mixture again and cook in hot bacon fat. Keep over hot fire, turning at least twice until fish is golden brown. Cooking time depends on size of fish, but is generally 10 to 15 minutes. Lay bacon over fish to serve. To make a real western meal, serve with sourdough bread.

Serves 6.

Skillet Cooked Fish

The most popular way to cook fish is still one of the least healthy: pan-frying. However, you can make it a little healthier by foregoing the bacon fat or drippings of days past, and using an oil. We prefer an olive oil and follow the basic recipe below. If you can get good thick cuts of halibut, in particular, try cutting it into cubes or blocks and cooking this way.

Dredge 1 lb/500 g fish fillets in pepper-seasoned flour. In large skillet, heat 1 clove garlic in ⅓ cup/80 mL extra virgin olive oil. Remove garlic and sauté fish until brown and crusty on both sides. Sprinkle with oregano and squeeze lemon juice over fillets before serving.

Thai Rice, Crusty Tuna, Crisp Noodles & Lime

Our son sent this recipe home after a trip across Canada, knowing I'm always looking for new ideas. The way the rice is used in this dish is delicious.

¾ cup	rice, cooked	180 mL
1	small carrot, cut in fine julienne strips	1
1	sweet red pepper, cut in fine julienne strips	1
1	rib celery, thinly sliced	1
1	rib bok choy, thinly sliced	1
2 cups	mixed field greens	500 mL
2	naval oranges, peeled and segments separated	2
¾ cup	tamari or soy sauce	180 mL
1 tbsp	ginger, minced	15 mL
4	(6 oz/185 g each) fresh tuna fillets	4
2 tbsp	salad oil	30 mL
2 cups	fried chow mein noodles	500 mL
	Salt and pepper, if desired	
½ cup	Lime Dressing (recipe follows)	125 mL

Spread rice on baking sheet. Bake at 350°F/180°C until light brown, about 8 to 12 minutes. Cool. Place toasted rice in blender. Blend until consistency is like cornmeal and no whole rice grains remain. (This can be done ahead of time and rice refrigerated.)

Place vegetables, including mixed field greens, and oranges in serving dish and toss gently. If preparing ahead, cover and refrigerate to keep crisp.

Place ground rice in pie plate. In second pie plate, combine tamari and ginger. Dip tuna into tamari mixture (be sure to cover both sides), then into rice to coat both sides. Heat oil in heavy skillet until smoky hot. Lay fillets in pan and cook on both sides, to taste. They cook quickly, so should only take 3 to 4 minutes, depending on thickness. Do not overcook, as tuna tends to become dry.

When ready to serve, gently toss noodles into salad with lime dressing. Adjust seasoning to taste, with salt and pepper if desired. Divide salad among 4 chilled plates. Top each with tuna fillet and serve immediately.

Serves 4.

Lime Dressing:

2 tbsp	Thai fish sauce	30 mL
¼ cup	rice wine vinegar	60 mL
1 tbsp	soy sauce	15 mL
¼ cup	fresh lime juice	60 mL
2 tsp	ginger, freshly grated	10 mL
1 tbsp	shallot, finely chopped	15 mL
1 tsp	cilantro, finely chopped	5 mL
½ tsp	mint, chopped	2 mL
1 tsp	garlic, chopped	5 mL
2 tsp	basil, chopped	10 mL

Combine ingredients, mixing well. Refrigerate any leftover dressing to use with salads.

Makes approximately 1 cup/250 mL.

Sensational Sauces & Toppers

Fish that has been poached, baked, microwaved, boiled, pan-fried or barbecued can be dressed up with a sauce. Whether the sauces are hot or cold, they bring tantalizing new flavours to your dinner table with minimal effort. Many shellfish also "marry" well with sauces. A good topper or sauce makes meal preparation a cinch. Just practise basic cooking methods until you are completely confident in them, add a repertoire of sauces, and you will receive a chorus of admiration.

Tomato Coulis

This delicious tomato sauce can be made up and bottled for future use. For a fast meal, serve it on cooked pasta or rice with a can of tuna, salmon or shrimp. It is also good on top of a salmon pâté or served as a sauce with grilled fish.

2 tbsp	olive oil	30 mL
2	cloves garlic, crushed	2
1	can (24 oz/796 mL) tomatoes	1
½ tsp	salt	2 mL
½ tsp	black pepper, freshly ground	2 mL
1 tbsp	sugar	15 mL
1 tbsp	thyme	15 mL
1 tbsp	basil	15 mL

Heat olive oil in saucepan big enough to hold tomatoes. Add garlic; sauté 2 to 3 minutes, being careful not to brown. Add tomatoes, salt, pepper, sugar, thyme and basil. Cook uncovered on low heat for 1 hour, or until sauce thickens. Bottle in sterilized jar or bottle.

For a classy table presentation, pour into wine or fancy bottle. Personalize by adding a dribble of red wine, or herbs.

Makes approximately 2½ cups/625 mL.

Szechuan Sauce

3 tbsp	soy sauce	45 mL
1 tbsp	mild sesame oil	15 mL
3 tbsp	green onion, finely chopped	45 mL
1 tbsp	fresh ginger, chopped	15 mL
2	cloves garlic, minced	2
½ tsp	sugar	2 mL
¼ tsp	Tabasco sauce	1 mL

Combine ingredients and serve with fish or poultry.

Makes approximately ½ cup/125 mL.

Herbed Sauce

L ike tartar sauce, this herbed sauce is delicious with hot or cold cooked fish.

½ cup	mayonnaise	125 mL
½ cup	sour cream	125 mL
2 tbsp	sweet pickle, finely chopped	30 mL
1 tbsp	green onion, sliced	15 mL
1 tbsp	parsley, minced	15 mL
½ tsp	dry mustard	2 mL
½ tsp	paprika	2 mL
¼ tsp	salt (optional)	1 mL
	Pepper, to taste (optional)	

Combine all ingredients. Cover and chill.

Makes 1¼ cups/310 mL, enough for 4 to 6 servings.

Dilled Tomato Sauce

¼ cup	onion, chopped	60 mL
½ tsp	dried dillweed	2 mL
	or 1 tbsp/15 mL fresh dillweed	
1 tbsp	butter or margarine	15 mL
1	can (7½ oz/213 g) crushed tomatoes	1
3 tbsp	chili sauce	45 mL

Cook onion and dill in butter until onion is tender. Stir in undrained tomatoes and chili sauce. Bring to boil; reduce heat to simmer for 5 to 7 minutes.

Makes 1½ cups/375 mL, enough for 4 servings.

Lemon Garlic Oil

My favourite oil, Lemon Garlic Oil, came from my friends Nicole Paradise and Diane Savoie. They operate a booth at the Charlottetown Farmers Market in Prince Edward Island, where they sell the most wonderful French pastries, breads and other delicacies. Every so often we team up with our pasta-making buddy Denise Arsenault and put on a series of cooking classes.

3	garlic cloves	3
½	lemon, cut in 3 wedges, seeds removed	½
	Extra virgin olive oil	
	Bamboo skewers	

Use bamboo skewer to pierce garlic clove and add lemon slice, alternating. Place skewer in bottle and fill with oil. Use to marinate grilled fish or chicken, drizzle over vegetables or toss with fresh cooked pasta.

Lemon Garlic Sauce

½ cup	green onions, sliced	125 mL
2	cloves garlic, minced	2
¼ tsp	dried dillweed or tarragon, crushed	1 mL
1 tbsp	olive oil	15 mL
2 tbsp	all purpose flour	30 mL
1 cup	fish broth or chicken broth*	250 mL
⅓ cup	dairy sour cream	80 mL
½ tsp	lemon peel, grated	2 mL
¼ tsp	salt (optional)*	1 mL

* If using a commercial powder or bouillon cube for broth, you should taste before adding salt, as these preparations do contain salt.

In saucepan, cook onion, garlic, and herb in oil until onion is tender. Stir in 1 tbsp/15 mL flour. Add broth. Stir other tbsp flour into sour cream. Add lemon peel; stir mixture into broth. Add salt, if desired. Cook until bubbly; then cook 1 minute more. Serve hot with fish.

Makes 1⅓ cups/330 mL.

Tangy Tartar Sauce

Once you taste this lively condiment you may never open one of those little plastic containers again!

1 cup	mayonnaise	250 mL
¼ tsp	Tabasco sauce	1 mL
1 tsp	vinegar	5 mL
1 tbsp	onion, minced	15 mL
1 tbsp	parsley, chopped	15 mL
1 tbsp	capers, chopped	15 mL
2 tbsp	pickle, chopped	30 mL

Mix well. Refrigerate unused portion.

Makes 1¼ cups/310 mL.

Green Sauce

1 cup	fresh parsley sprigs, packed	250 mL
1 cup	fresh watercress leaves, packed	250 mL
1 cup	fresh basil leaves, packed	250 mL
¼ cup	pine nuts or toasted almonds	60 mL
¼ cup	fresh lime juice	60 mL
¼ cup	olive oil	60 mL
2	cloves garlic, chopped	2
½ tsp	Tabasco sauce	2 mL

Place all ingredients in food processor and process until smooth. Transfer to glass container; cover and chill 24 hours to develop flavour. Serve with hot or cold fish.

Makes about 1 cup/250 mL, enough for 16 servings.

Calypso Sauce

½ cup	light brown sugar	125 mL
¼ cup	lime juice	60 mL
2 tbsp	rum	30 mL
1 tsp	ground ginger	5 mL
2	cloves garlic, minced	2
¼ tsp	salt	1 mL
¼ tsp	Tabasco sauce	1 mL
⅛ tsp	ground cloves	0.5 mL

Combine all ingredients in glass measuring cup. Microwave on high 45 seconds to 1 minute. Serve with shrimp or prawns.

Makes approximately 1 cup/250 mL.

Red Pepper Relish

1	jar (7 oz/198 g) roasted red peppers, drained and diced	1
20	olives, pitted and chopped	20
1 tsp	extra virgin olive oil	5 mL
1 tsp	balsamic vinegar	5 mL
1	small clove garlic, minced	1
¾ tsp	fresh oregano leaves, minced	7 mL
½ tsp	fresh lemon juice	5 mL
Pinch	dried red pepper flakes	Pinch

Mix all ingredients together in small bowl. Serve at room temperature.

Makes approximately 1 cup/250 mL.

Great Grillers

Grilled Seafood

With the introduction of electric tabletop barbecues and stone grills, grilling has become a year-round favourite method of cooking, even in cold northern climates. Fish and shellfish both work wonderfully well on the grill. The brave among us learn how to prepare just about anything on the barbecue — even seafood pizza.

Grilling

Once considered an elementary method of cooking, grilling has evolved into a global style of food preparation that allows for recipes both casual and sophisticated. Whether your grill is on an apartment balcony, in a backyard, or is a portable one that you carry in the car trunk, it can be the focal point of many favourite meals.

New inspiration is finding its way into the meals of many cooks who use grilling. Influences such as Indonesian satays, Asian-inspired teriyaki, Tex Mex fajitas and Middle Eastern shish kebabs combine with our own cookouts on the shore to bring seafood over the coals into the limelight. Chefs will tell you that customers are asking for more and more grilled foods — for many people, it has become the culmination of their culinary expertise.

Mastering the techniques of grilling requires practice, vigilance and insightful decision making. The challenge, according to Jay Solomon, chef and owner of *Jay's Cafe* at Clinton Hall in Ithica, N.Y., is to "sear and seal." That is, sear the product while sealing in the juices and strive to produce optimal flavour without overcooking or undercooking. The proper grilling temperature, timing and a well-seasoned grill contribute to a good final product. If a grill temperature is too low, the food will have to remain on the grill longer, and, especially in the case of seafood, will dry out. If the heat is too high, the outside will char and the inside will be left raw.

Personally, I feel the key to success is to know your grill: where the hot and warm spots are; what temperature works best in which weather conditions and so on. And remember that grilling is a state of mind that encompasses good friends and good food.

Tips for Grillers

- Select fish with firm flesh and strong flavours, such as salmon, tuna, swordfish, catfish, mahimahi, redfish and halibut. Shellfish such as shrimps, scallops, mussels, lobster, and even clams also grill well. Flaky fish, such as Boston Bluefish, haddock and orange roughy, tend to fall apart on a grill, so cook them in a fish basket designed for the task.

- Lightly coat the cold, clean grill rack with non-stick cooking spray for easy clean-up.

- Preheat your barbecue. If using charcoal, allow 25 to 30 minutes for it to become hot. Resist cooking until coals are ash grey. At night they will glow red.

- Always clean the grill after using. Not only is food safety a factor, but you will reduce sticking and build up left by the oils used for basting or in marinades. How you clean depends on the type of grill. Our gas barbecue has porcelain grills which we brush off with a brush, then put in the dishwasher. I love it! Follow the manufacturer's instructions for best results.

- Always think ahead. Seafood grills quickly, so have the rest of the meal ready (salads made, potatoes baked, veggies on the grill), the table set and drinks ready to pour before starting to cook. Seafood also cools quickly and in most cases should be enjoyed hot. Serving plates can be warmed on the top shelf of your barbecue or, if there is likely to be any delay, put cooked seafood on a serving plate and cover with a wok or cake lid to keep it warm.

- Have some fun trying wood chips such as mesquite, cherry, hickory and apple, for unique flavours. Alder complements fish, as do whole branches of herbs such as thyme, oregano, dill and fennel. When soaked in water they can be applied straight to the coals.

- A few years ago, "blackening" was all the rage. I love the taste but would never recommend it for the home cook because the smoke makes an awful mess of the kitchen. However, a very similar taste can be obtained by sprinkling cajun seasonings over fish while it is being grilled. This method eliminates the fat used in blackening, so it is healthier. You can buy cajun seasoning mix, or try creating your own seasoning combinations such as cumin, coriander, chili powder and cayenne pepper. Rub the seasoning into seafood before placing on the grill. Give it a squeeze of fresh lime juice and voilà — a masterpiece.

- Marinades give flavour to fish, as well as tenderizing and keeping it from drying out. There are many marinades recommended in this chapter, or you may use a mildly seasoned blend of soy sauce and garlic to add flavour without overpowering the fish. Allow fish to rest in marinade in the refrigerator for 25 to 30 minutes and then brush it on during cooking to retain moisture. If preparing a marinade with oil, use olive or vegetable to prevent sticking to the grill.

- Brush seafood with oil and rub in commercial blends of seasoning. For instance, jerk barbecuing, the Jamaican way of marinating and grilling, works well with fish. The highly seasoned marinade features thyme, green onions, cloves, allspice, soy, vinegar and chili peppers. You can now buy Jamaican Jerk seasoning. Sprinkle it on fish that has been brushed with olive oil, and then rub in. You can also rub in Italian seasoning mix, dill, lemon pepper, herb and spice mixes — the choice today is almost unlimited.

- When grilling fish steaks, such as salmon steaks, cut a slice of lemon, orange or zucchini the same size as the cavity made by cleaning. Place in the "hole" and wrap the thinner legs of the steak around it. Use toothpicks to secure the fish to the fruit or vegetable. Squeeze juice over the fish, brush with oil — or use a complementary marinade — and grill.

Sauces & Marinades

There are important distinctions between grilling sauces and grilling marinades.

Sauces are liquid seasonings applied to food either before or during eating. Never put red tomato or sweet barbecue sauces on food before or during the cooking process. Tomato-based and sweetened barbecue sauces tend to burn and should be used during final basting, or served alongside the cooked product. Application during the last minutes of cooking seals moisture and provides flavour, but it is a wise idea only if the fire is low and you prefer a bit of charring on the outside. When cooking fish or shellfish, the cooking time is shorter than meat — and seafood is much more delicate to work with. That is why you seldom see commercial sauces of the type described recommended for fish.

Marinades are liquid seasoning mixtures in which foods are immersed before cooking. They usually consist of an acidic ingredient like vinegar, citrus juice or wine which penetrates and tenderizes meat or seafood fibres, and oil which moistens the meat and carries the flavour throughout the flesh. Prepare marinades in a non-aluminium bowl to avoid a reaction between the aluminium and the acidic ingredient. Control the intensity of flavour by varying the marinating time. Seafood usually requires much less time than meat because it takes in the flavour and tenderizing attributes much more quickly. Generally, vegetables and fish require minimal time — just 20 minutes. Compare that to poultry, which is best marinated for 30 minutes, and beef, pork and lamb, which can marinate for up to 2 hours.

When I'm having a seafood barbecue, I usually prepare the marinade and vegetables or side dishes, pour the marinade over the seafood (and vegetables, if grilling) and light the barbecue. By the time I have the table set, the barbecue is heated and the seafood ready for cooking. As it takes only minutes to cook, we sit down to dinner at the table ½ hour after preparations began. If you are grilling vegetables, remember they may need to go on the grill before the seafood.

Delicate fish such as sole, scallops and flounder shine with only a simple butter or light sauce. Richer fish, like salmon, swordfish and tuna, benefit from a flavourful marinade before grilling.

Oriental Grilled Shrimp with Peanut Dipping Sauce

These shrimp, prepared with the shell on, make great finger food for hot nights on the deck watching the fireflies, listening to the frogs sing, sipping on a long cool one and pickin' and shellin' as conversation rolls around. Easy-peel shrimp are sold by seafood retailers today. Their shell has been split down the back and deveined for easy use. You can do this yourself with a pair of kitchen shears.

1 tbsp	lite soy sauce	15 mL
1 tbsp	lemon juice	15 mL
1 tsp	sesame oil	5 mL
½ tsp	fresh ginger, grated	2 mL
1 lb	large shrimp, shell on	500 g
1 tbsp	sesame seeds (optional)	15 mL
	Peanut Dipping Sauce (recipe follows)	

Combine soy sauce, lemon juice, sesame oil and ginger. Pour over shrimp and marinate 1 hour. Thread shrimp on skewers, pushing skewer through both head and tail end of each shrimp. Sprinkle with sesame seeds.

Place skewers on oiled grill rack over hot coals, or under broiler; cook about 3 minutes each side. Slide shrimp off skewers to serve. Remove shells and dip in peanut sauce.

Serves 4.

Peanut Dipping Sauce:

¼ cup	creamy peanut butter	60 mL
⅓ cup	water	80 mL
¼ tsp	curry powder	2 mL
1 tbsp	honey	15 mL
1 tbsp	lemon juice	15 mL
1 tbsp	lite soy sauce	15 mL

Combine all ingredients, stirring until smooth.

Grilled Lobster with Lime & Tequila Baste

Raw or precooked lobster is delicious on the barbecue if carefully cooked. Remember that precooked lobster only needs to be heated, so should not remain over the coals more than one or two minutes.

Lobsters (allow 1-2 each)
Lime Tequila Baste (recipe follows)

Split lobster from head to tail and crack claws and knuckles. Place in Lime Tequila Baste. Oil or spray cold grills with non-stick cooking spray. Preheat coals.

Place lobster shell-side-down on coals. Baste before turning. Raw lobster will take 3 to 7 minutes to cook, depending on temperature and size of lobster. Precooked lobster only needs to be heated and lightly browned on meat side. Place shell-side-down for 1 to 2 minutes; baste and turn over. Drizzle with remaining Lime Tequila Baste before serving.

Lime & Tequila Baste:

½ cup	lime juice (4 limes), fresh squeezed	125 mL
2 tbsp	tequila	30 mL
1	clove garlic, minced	1
¾ tsp	Tabasco sauce	7 mL
¼ cup	fresh coriander, chopped	60 mL
½ cup	olive oil	125 mL
	Salt and pepper, to taste	

In small non-aluminum bowl, combine first 5 ingredients. Gradually add olive oil and stir after each addition. Add salt and pepper, to taste.

Makes approximately 1 cup/250 mL.

Grilled Monkfish

This ugly fish is commonly known as the "Angler Fish" because of the way it lures its next meal by burying itself in the sand and then dangling what looks like a worm to entice the unwary within snapping distance. It is sometimes also called the "sea devil." The flavour is sometimes compared to lobster — in fact, the Spaniards are known to call it "poor man's lobster." Try it — you'll like it.

6	(8 oz/250 g each) fillets monkfish	6
1 cup	olive oil	250 mL
1 tbsp	mustard powder	15 mL
½ tsp	tarragon powder	2 mL
	Juice of 1 lemon	
1	garlic clove, crushed	1
1 tbsp	dry sherry	15 mL
	Salt and pepper, to taste	

Mix all ingredients in casserole dish and marinate fish overnight in refrigerator. To grill, cook 15 minutes each side, using some marinade to baste while cooking.

Serves 6.

Grilled Tuna Quesadillas

Quesadillas, or Mexican "turnovers," are great barbecue treats. For a quick meal, they can be made with any precooked seafood such as tuna, salmon, shrimp, lobster or crab. Serve with a salad of fancy greens, cherry tomato wedges and a vinaigrette dressing. For a variation, substitute refried beans spread with sour cream and guacamole instead of the bean/salsa mix.

1	can (19 oz/540 mL) kidney beans, rinsed and drained	1
1 cup	salsa	250 mL
4	10-inch/25-cm flour tortillas	4
1	can (7½ oz/213 g) flaked tuna, or other seafood cut into small pieces	1
4	green onions, chopped	4
¼ cup	green olives, chopped	60 mL
2 tbsp	fresh coriander or parsley, chopped	30 mL
1 cup	extra-old Cheddar cheese, shredded	250 mL
⅓ cup	Monterey Jack cheese, shredded	80 mL
	Salsa, as garnish	

Mash beans with potato masher and combine with salsa. Divide mixture between 4 tortillas, laid flat. Spread evenly, leaving ½ inch/1 cm border all around. Sprinkle with seafood, onions, olives, coriander and cheeses, in that order. Fold tortilla over and press edges gently together.

Barbecue tortillas on greased grill over medium-high heat for 8 to 10 minutes or until browned and crisped; turn halfway through cooking. Serve with salad and remaining salsa on side.

Serves 4.

Peanut Sauce for Skewers

A t *Sinclair's Grill* in Jupiter, Florida, large shrimp are alternated on skewers
with veggie chunks such as yellow and red peppers, green onions or water
chestnuts and served with a spicy peanut sauce. Loop a snow pea around
scallops for a nice presentation. This recipe makes 1 qt/1 L of sauce for skewers,
so would be good for a barbecue for friends. If not serving a crowd, halve or
quarter the recipe.

¾ inch	piece ginger root, pared and minced	2 cm
¼	garlic head, pared and crushed	¼
1 lb	creamy peanut butter	500 mL
¼ cup	chicken stock	60 mL
2 tbsp	light soy sauce	30 mL
1 tbsp	chili oil	15 mL
2 tbsp	honey	30 mL
2 tbsp	cilantro leaves, chopped	30 mL
	Salt and pepper, to taste	
	Lime juice, to taste	

Combine all but last 2 ingredients. Mix well and season with lime juice and salt
and pepper, to taste. Store in sealed container until ready to use.

Makes 1 qt/1 L sauce.

Tandoori-Grilled Tuna

Tandoori is an Indian method of marinating and roasting chicken or fish in a tandoori oven. Chef Jay Solomon of *Jay's Cafe* in Ithaca, N.Y. has transformed this technique into a grilled item on his menu. He tenderizes the tuna and imparts a delicate, smoky flavour with a hint of fire.

1½ lb	fresh tuna steaks, cut ½ inch/1 cm thick	750 g
	Marinade (recipe follows)	

Prepare marinade. Place tuna steaks in shallow dish and cover with marinade. Refrigerate 4 hours, turning fish once. Preheat grill until coals are grey to white. Raise grill at least 6 inches/15 cm from heat. Remove tuna from marinade and pat dry. Lightly oil grill and place tuna steaks over heat. Turn after 5 to 7 minutes. Continue grilling another 5 minutes or until tuna is pale brown or burgundy in centre. Serve immediately with fruit chutney, relish or mustard sauce.

Serves 4.

Marinade:

2 cups	plain yogurt	500 mL
½ cup	olive oil	125 mL
¼ cup	red wine vinegar	60 mL
2 tbsp	ginger root, minced	30 mL
10-12	garlic cloves, minced	10-12
1-2	jalapeño peppers, seeded and minced	1-2
2 tbsp	ground cumin	30 mL
2 tbsp	ground coriander	30 mL
1 tbsp	paprika	15 mL
1 tsp	ground clove	5 mL
1 tsp	black pepper	5 mL
1 tsp	salt	5 mL
1 tsp	red hot sauce	5 mL
½ tsp	cayenne pepper	2 mL

Grilled Smoked Salmon on Corn Blinis

(with Buckwheat Sprouts, Summer Squash Relish and Chipotle Chili Crema)

Chef Lawrence Nangay of *The Chef's Table Catering* in Barrie, Ontario created this super griller. We had the Chef's salmon served with Corn Blinis and Summer Squash Relish and are happy to be able to present it to you as it was presented to us. My companion of the day dubbed the experience "grazer grilling" because the appetizer portions were served hot off the grill to eager folks who just stood around waiting for them to be ready. Think about that kind of informal serving for your own barbecue. There are many specialty ingredients recommended below, so check all four recipes carefully.

Once you have prepared the four recipes below, follow these instructions for assembling:

Lightly grill salmon to warm through, then cut into 10 to 12 pieces. Top warm blini with 2 tbsp/30 mL buckwheat sprouts and 1 tbsp/15 mL of relish. Place 1 piece of warm salmon on top; put dollop of crema on salmon.

Serves 4.

Grilled Smoked Salmon:
This salmon is exceptional by itself, served with a simple side dish like our Dill Cucumber Sauce (see index).

1 lb	boneless salmon fillet	500 g
1 tsp	coarse salt	5 mL
1 tsp	cracked white peppercorns	5 mL

Lay salmon skin side down and rub in salt and pepper. If using kettle or rectangular grill with cover, smoke salmon over indirect heat. Centre salmon over drip pan, skin side down; close cover and smoke 1 hour, or until internal temperature reaches 140°F/60°C. Apple wood chips are ideal for smoking salmon.

Corn Blinis:

Blinis hail from Russia, where the small pancakes are classically served with sour cream and smoked salmon or caviar. When we had them, the griddle was placed right over coals on a barbecue so that they could be quickly assembled with warm salmon. Delicious!

½ cup	cornmeal	125 mL
½ cup	all purpose flour	125 mL
1 tbsp	baking powder	15 mL
1 tsp	salt	5 mL
1	egg, slightly beaten	1
1¼ cups	milk	310 mL
1 tbsp	butter, melted	15 mL

In mixing bowl combine cornmeal, flour, baking powder and salt. In separate bowl, combine egg, milk and butter. Lightly butter hot griddle.

Just before cooking, pour liquid ingredients into dry ingredients; lightly mix to blend. Using ⅓ cup/80 mL batter for each blini, cook blinis on griddle. Remove to warm plate.

Summer Squash Relish:

1	small zucchini, finely diced	1
1	small yellow summer squash, finely diced	1
1	medium tomato, finely diced	1
½ cup	roasted corn	125 mL
1	clove garlic, finely chopped	1
½	small red onion	½
1 tbsp	fresh marjoram, finely chopped	15 mL
1	serrano chili, seeded and finely chopped	1
4 tsp	extra virgin olive oil	20 mL
1 tbsp	balsamic vinegar	15 mL
	Sugar, to taste	
	Salt, to taste	

Combine all ingredients. Let sit at room temperature at least 1 hour before serving.

See over for Chipotle Chili Cream.

Chipotle Chili Cream:

½ cup	30% cream	125 mL
1 tbsp	buttermilk	15 mL
1	clove garlic, roasted and peeled	1
1 tbsp	chipotle chilies, canned in adobo sauce	15 mL

Heat cream in saucepan to warm. Pour into clean container. Add buttermilk. Cover with cheesecloth, and place overnight in warm location to set. Purée cream with garlic and chipotle. Leave at room temperature.

Seafood Satay

A n ancient method of skewering and marinating shellfish or meats, satay is said to be the backyard barbecue of Indonesia. Satays are often threaded on a skewer, grilled and served with a spicy condiment (satay sauce). We like the Indonesian Peanut Sauce. Most versions of satay include soy or fish sauce, lime juice, peanut butter, coconut milk, vinegar, lemon grass and chili peppers or pastes. The ingredients listed below form a warm, aromatic alliance of flavours. The recipe has been adapted from one by Jay Solomon of *Jay's Cafe* in Ithaca, N.Y.

2 cups	coconut milk	500 mL
¼ cup	rice wine vinegar	60 mL
1	fresh lemon grass stalk, minced *or* 1 tbsp/15 mL lime zest	1
1-2 tsp	chili-garlic paste (available where Asian foods are sold)	5-10 mL
2 tbsp	fresh cilantro, minced	30 mL
1 lb	prawns, scallops or firm-fleshed fish such as tuna, cut into chunks	500 g
	Indonesian Peanut Sauce (recipe follows)	

Combine coconut milk, vinegar, lemon grass, chili paste and cilantro in mixing bowl. Thread seafood onto 10-inch-long metal or bamboo skewers* and place in rectangular dish. Pour marinade over skewers and refrigerate 20 minutes, turning once or twice.

Have rest of meal ready to serve before cooking begins. Preheat grill until coals are grey to white. When coals are ready, place skewers on grill. Turn once during cooking. Cooking time will be 3 to 5 minutes, depending on size of seafood. Cook until fish or scallops are opaque, and shrimps pink. Serve immediately with Indonesian Peanut Sauce.

Serves 3 to 4.

* If using bamboo skewers, soak in water for 10 minutes before threading.

Indonesian Peanut Sauce:

1½ tsp	peanut oil	7 mL
1	small onion, diced	1
1	clove garlic, minced	1
½	chili pepper, seeded and minced	½
1½ tsp	fresh lemon grass, minced	7 mL
2 tbsp	soy sauce or fish sauce	30 mL
1 tbsp	brown sugar	15 mL
1 tbsp	lime juice	15 mL
¾ cup	coconut milk	180 mL
½ tsp	ground coriander	2 mL
½ tsp	ground cumin	2 mL
½ cup	chunky peanut butter	125 mL
1 tbsp	fresh cilantro, minced	15 mL

Heat peanut oil in skillet over medium-high heat. Sauté onion, garlic, chili pepper and lemon grass, about 4 minutes. Stir in soy sauce, brown sugar, lime juice, coconut milk, coriander and cumin. Thoroughly blend peanut butter into mixture.

Bring sauce to simmer over low heat, stirring frequently. Stir in cilantro and remove from heat. Serve at once with satay, or refrigerate.

Eastern Shore Swordfish

2	lemons	2
3 lb	swordfish or bluefish steaks	1.5 kg
¼ cup	mayonnaise	60 mL
¾ tsp	Tabasco sauce	3 mL
6 tbsp	unsalted butter or margarine, softened	90 mL
3 tbsp	fresh parsley, chopped	45 mL
	Dried seaweed for coals (optional)	

Prepare coals for grilling. Cut 1 lemon in half and rub each side of steaks with juice. In small bowl, blend mayonnaise and Tabasco sauce. Brush onto both sides of steaks. Grill both sides of steaks until just cooked through, about 6 minutes each side, depending on thickness of steaks. Remove from grill and spread with butter. Sprinkle with parsley and serve with remaining lemon, cut into wedges.

Serves 6.

Swordfish with Rosemary

This recipe is especially good for portable tabletop grills and rangetop models. Set the temperature at medium hot, place the grate as far away from the heat as possible, and preheat.

2	(about 6 oz/185 g each) swordfish or halibut steaks, cut 1 inch/2.5 cm thick (thaw if frozen)	2
2 tbsp	olive or cooking oil	30 mL
2 tbsp	white-wine vinegar	30 mL
1	green onion, thinly sliced	1
½ tsp	dried rosemary, crushed	2 mL
¼ tsp	salt (optional)	1 mL

Combine oil, vinegar, onion, rosemary and salt in shallow dish. Add fish and marinate 1 hour at room temperature. Drain, reserving marinade. Grill fish 5 to 7 minutes per side, brushing often with marinade.

Serves 2.

Saucy Grilled Northern Shark

This recipe works well for halibut, swordfish, ocean catfish, cask, code, hake, Atlantic salmon and shark, as well as Northern shark (also sold as dogfish).

2 tbsp	sugar	30 mL
1 tbsp	vinegar	15 mL
½ cup	chicken broth	125 mL
2 tbsp	orange juice concentrate	30 mL
1 tsp	orange rind, grated	5 mL
1 cup	water	250 mL
2 tbsp	cornstarch	30 mL
2 lb	(6 steaks) Northern shark steaks (or see suggestion above)	1 kg
¼ cup	vegetable, olive or peanut oil	60 mL

Oil grill and preheat to high. Combine sugar and vinegar in small saucepan. Heat until sugar begins to caramelize. Add chicken broth; stir until dissolved. Stir in orange juice, rind and cornstarch diluted in water. Cook, stirring until thickened. Place pan on back of barbecue or stove to keep warm.

Meanwhile, place steaks on grill (if using fillets, place in oiled, wire grill baskets) and cook over high heat, 4 to 5 minutes both sides, until flesh is opaque. Baste frequently with oil. Serve with orange sauce. Garnish with orange slices, if desired.

Serves 6.

Texas Bite for Grilled Fish

Many people interested in cutting fat and calories are turning to the cooking styles of the southern United States. Fish in this recipe is simply brushed with butter or oil and grilled, then served with a dollop of wonderful salsa straight from Texas.

Fish fillets or steaks suitable for grilling
Olive oil
Texas Bite Salsa (recipe follows)

Oil grill or wire fish basket. Heat grill to medium hot. Brush fish with oil and place on grill, turning halfway through grilling time; cook only until fish flakes easily with fork. Fish tends to dry out fast when cooked over flame, so brush lightly with oil or a little butter to keep moist. Serve immediately with Texas Bite Salsa.

Texas Bite Salsa:

If you prefer to use dried black beans, follow the recipe on the package and cook and cool before starting. Choose the largest, heaviest sweet red pepper you can find.

1	large sweet red pepper	1
1 cup	canned black beans, rinsed and drained	250 mL
1 tsp	salt	5 mL
1½ cups	thick, tomato-based, bottled hot salsa	375 mL
1½ cups	corn kernels, well drained (thaw if frozen)	375 mL
4	green onions, chopped	4
½ cup	cilantro, minced	125 mL

Place red pepper on barbecue over flame, or under broiler, or in flame of gas burner; roast, turning often until pepper is charred black all over. Cool until pepper can be handled, then rub or peel away black peel. Remove stem and core.

Chop flesh into small pieces and combine with other ingredients, stirring in cilantro last. Cover and refrigerate at least 1 hour before serving.

Makes approximately 4 cups/1 L salsa.

Grilled Rainbow Trout with Chili & Almond Pesto

This makes more pesto than you will need to serve six, so increase the amount of fish, if you wish. Refrigerate unused pesto.

4-6	ancho or Anaheim chilies (about 8 oz/250 g total), roasted *or* 1 cup/250 mL canned roasted peppers	4-6
¼ cup	toasted almonds, blanched and slivered	60 mL
⅓ cup	olive oil	80 mL
3	cloves garlic	3
6	Rainbow trout, boned, head removed, butterfly cut*	6
6 tbsp	orange juice	90 mL
	Toasted almonds, sliced, for garnish	
	Cilantro, for garnish	

* Trout skin is left on and the backbone and pin bones are removed. If boned fish is not available, or if you can't manage to remove the bones and leave the fish intact, use 2 fillets for each serving.

In food processor, blend chilies with almonds, olive oil and garlic to make pesto. Oil grill and preheat barbecue or grill. Sprinkle trout with juice and grill 4 minutes or until trout turns opaque.

Place on hot plates and top with chili pesto (use about ⅓ pesto and place rest on table for people to help themselves). Garnish with sliced almonds and cilantro. Serve immediately.

Serves 6.

Salmon Fillets

Salmon steaks or fillets are wonderful grilled with a basting sauce, such as this one, that keeps them moist and succulent. Although the recipe calls for mayonnaise, it works best with Miracle Whip. Extra sauce should be warmed and served on the side. We put the sauce in a small saucepan on the barbecue and use it for basting, then serve the remainder alongside the fish.

4-6	salmon steaks or fillets	4-6
	Jack's Basting Sauce (recipe follows)	

Oil or spray cold grills with non-stick cooking spray. Preheat barbecue. Brush sauce on both sides of salmon and grill 5 to 6 inches/12 to 15 cm above coats until browned. Turn over and brush with sauce again. Cook until fish flakes easily with fork. Serve with remaining basting liquid, warm, on side.

Serves 4.

Jack's Basting Sauce:

⅔ cup	mayonnaise (see note above)	160 mL
⅓ cup	butter or margarine, melted	80 mL
1 tbsp	white vinegar	15 mL
1 tbsp	liquid honey	15 mL
½ tsp	dried dillweed	2 mL
1 tbsp	lemon juice, freshly squeezed	15 mL
	Lemon pepper, to taste	
	Salt, to taste	

Combine all ingredients. Mix until smooth.

Smoked Splake

This dish was first sampled at the "Feast of the Fields" event in Ontario, where some of the region's finest chefs gather to promote organic food, their own establishments and good eating. Roman Trutiak of *Grant's Spike and Spoon* in Collingwood, Ontario served this wonderful fish with Dill, Cucumber and Yogurt Sauce (see index). Roman says, "Organic farming is here to stay and we as chefs should, whenever possible, support this natural alternative." The method of smoking described here also works for other types of fish.

1	bunch dill	1
4 tbsp	cracked black peppercorns	60 mL
⅔ cup	pickling salt	160 mL
7 tbsp	sugar	105 mL
2	fresh splake fillets (2-3 lb/1-1.5 kg), bones removed, skin left on	2
1	home smoker	1

Roughly chop dill, reserving a few sprigs for making sauce or to use as garnish. Crack black peppercorns and mix pickling salt and sugar together.

Lay fillets side by side, flesh side up. Sprinkle layer of salt mixture on fish, coating well. Then sprinkle black peppercorns evenly over fillets. Finally, coat fish with dill. Place first fillet on top of second; completely cover in plastic wrap and refrigerate overnight. Turn fish once after 8 hours, for even curing in brine.

The next day, unwrap fillets and gently remove all dill and cracked peppercorns. Rinse under cold water and pat dry. Let fish stand uncovered and dry 1 hour, to form light skin. Place fillets on top rack of smoker and gently smoke for 6 to 8 hours. Serve with Dill Cucumber Sauce (see index).

Serves 8 as an appetizer, 4 as a main course.

Barbecued Whole Salmon

The trick of cooking whole salmon on the barbecue is knowing how to handle it. While these directions are for a Pacific salmon, they are useful for any whole fish.

Rinse salmon under cold running water and pat dry inside and out. Sprinkle cavity with salt, pepper and lemon juice. If desired, stuff lightly (stuffing recipe follows), skewer and lace closed.

Rub generously with softened butter. Tear off double thickness of heavy duty foil that is equal in length, and at least twice the width, of salmon. Oil foil on 1 side. Punch numerous pencil holes through foil. Over hot coals, place foil flat on grill, oiled side up.

Place salmon on foil. Measure at thickest point. Allow 12 to 15 minutes per inch/2.5 cm total cooking time. Halfway through cooking time, gather long edges of foil together to form "handle." Grip handle, flip salmon; reopen foil for rest of cooking time. Test with fork for doneness along both sides of backbone at thickest point. Juices should run clear and flesh should be opaque.

For oven baking, measure at thickest point, including stuffing, and bake at 450°F/230°C for 10 minutes per inch/2.5 cm thickness, or until juices run clear and flesh and flesh fork-tested along backbone is opaque.

Summer Gardening Stuffing:
Here is sufficient stuffing for a whole salmon, approximately 3 lb/1.5 kg, cooked as above.

½ cup	potato, cooked, finely chopped	125 mL
¼ cup	tomato, finely chopped	60 mL
¼ cup	cucumber, finely chopped	60 mL
2 tbsp	green pepper, finely chopped	30 mL
2 tbsp	onion, finely chopped	30 mL
4 oz	shrimp or crab meat (optional)	125 g
2 tsp	lemon juice	10 mL
1 tsp	fresh dill, finely chopped	5 mL
	Salt and pepper, to taste	
1 tbsp	butter, melted	15 mL

Combine all ingredients, tossing gently but thoroughly. Stuff salmon cavity lightly. Any remaining stuffing may be wrapped in foil and cooked alongside salmon. Cook as above.

Makes 1½ cups/375 mL.

Kahlua Lime Marinade for Fish

This marinade is good for any fish you want to bake or barbecue.

½ cup	Kahlua	125 mL
¼ cup	fresh lime juice (about 2 limes)	60 mL
2 tbsp	vegetable oil	30 mL
1 tsp	ginger, freshly grated	5 mL
6	dashes Tabasco sauce	6
¼ tsp	white pepper	1 mL
¼ tsp	dried dill weed	1 mL

Shake all ingredients together in covered jar. Let stand 1 hour or longer to blend flavours. Shake well before using. Baste fish on both sides and marinate 30 minutes. Baste once or twice during barbecuing or baking.

Makes ¾ cup/180 mL.

Miami Marinade

½ cup	lime juice (about 4 limes)	125 mL
4 tbsp	sesame seeds	60 mL
4 tbsp	vegetable oil	60 mL
3 tbsp	soy sauce	45 mL
4	cloves garlic, minced	4
1 tsp	Tabasco sauce	5 mL

Combine all ingredients. Refrigerate until ready to use as marinade for fish or vegetables.

Makes 1 cup/250 mL.

Alaskan Seafood Marinade

8 tbsp	unsalted butter or margarine	120 mL
1 cup	brown sugar, packed	250 mL
⅓ cup	honey	80 mL
1 tbsp	fresh lemon juice	15 mL
1 tbsp	liquid smoke flavouring	15 mL
¼ tsp	dried rosemary	1 mL
1 tsp	Tabasco sauce	5 mL

In medium-size, non-aluminum saucepan over medium heat, combine all ingredients. Cook, stirring until smooth, 5 to 7 minutes. Cool to room temperature. Marinate seafood for 30 minutes prior to grilling.

Makes approximately 1 cup/250 mL.

Key West Lime & Tequila Baste

This recipe works well as a marinade for fish and shellfish.

½ cup	lime juice (about 4 limes), fresh squeezed	125 mL
2 tbsp	tequila	30 mL
1	clove garlic, minced	1
¾ tsp	Tabasco sauce	7 mL
¼ cup	fresh coriander, chopped	60 mL
½ cup	olive oil	125 mL
	Salt and pepper, to taste	

In small non-aluminum bowl, combine first 5 ingredients. Gradually add olive oil and stir after each addition. Salt and pepper, to taste. Reserve ¼ cup/60 mL and pour rest over fish or shellfish. Marinate for 20 minutes prior to cooking. When cooked, drizzle reserved marinade over fish before serving.

Makes 1½ cups/375 mL.

New Zealand Oreo Dory

1½ lb	(4-6 fillets) smooth oreo dory	750 g
¼ cup	lemon juice	60 mL
1 tbsp	Dijon mustard	15 mL
2 tbsp	barbecue sauce	30 mL
¼ tsp	Tabasco sauce	1 mL
¼ cup	tomato sauce	60 mL

Combine all ingredients except fish in jar with tight-fitting lid. Shake to mix thoroughly. Preheat barbecue, oiling cold grills before starting. Baste fish fillets with liquid. Barbecue over hot coals approximately 2 to 3 minutes each side.

Serves 4.

Lemon Marinated Smooth Oreo Dory

This recipe also works very well for baking fish. Place fillets in an ovenproof dish, pour marinade over and chill for one hour. Then place the dish four to five inches/ten to twelve cm from a preheated broiler during cooking. Broil three to four minutes on each side, basting with marinade during cooking.

1½ lb	(4-6 fillets) smooth oreo dory	750 g
3 tbsp	lemon juice	45 mL
1	clove garlic, crushed	1
1 tsp	ginger root, finely chopped	5 mL
1 tbsp	oil	15 mL

Combine all ingredients except fish in jar with tight-fitting lid. Shake to mix thoroughly. Place fillets in large shallow dish and pour marinade over all. Place in refrigerator 1 hour, turning once. Preheat barbecue. Oil wire fish-grilling basket and place fillets in it. Cook over high heat 3 to 5 minutes until fish is opaque, basting often with reserved marinade. Serve immediately.

Serves 4.

Cool Tempters

Salads

Although we may think of salads as an invention of health-conscious individuals in modern society, they have in fact been in the limelight since earliest recorded times. Salads with seafood are simple to prepare, brimming with nutrition and good health, fill many culinary roles and bring us wonderful flavour combinations.

Think Pink with Roses

Flowers have become an accepted part of culinary experience. Naysayers should take note: in addition to their visual appeal, flowers have a sweet, delicate taste which gives a whole new flavour to salad. This creation brings together tiny pink shrimp and the petals of pink roses.

3	heads Bibb lettuce, rinsed, drained and broken up	3
1	can (6½ oz/175 g) tiny cocktail shrimp	1
1	can (10 oz/284 mL) tiny orange segments, in their own juice, drained	1
3	pink sweetheart roses*, rinsed, drained and petals removed	3
2	bunches watercress, rinsed and drained	2
	Dressing (recipe follows)	

* Flowers should be unsprayed.

Prepare dressing. Arrange lettuce on 6 plates. Scatter shrimp, oranges and rose petals, dividing evenly; garnish with sprigs of watercress on each. Cover with plastic wrap and refrigerate until ready to serve.

When ready to serve, drizzle 2 to 3 tbsp/30 to 45 mL dressing over each plate and serve remainder of dressing at table.

Serves 6.

Dressing:

½ cup	lemon juice	125 mL
2 tsp	granulated sugar	10 mL
2 tsp	chives, finely chopped	10 mL
1 tsp	Dijon mustard	10 mL
½ tsp	salt	2 mL
	Pepper, to taste	
1 cup	vegetable oil	250 mL

Whisk together first 6 ingredients. Gradually whisk in oil.

Salad in Sourdough

R ound loaves of sourdough bread make wonderful holders for dips or salads. This recipe calls for two people to share a sourdough "bowl." However, if you wish to have individual servings, select smaller loaves, or use sourdough rolls. When using your "bowl" for a dip, you don't need to bake it.

2	round loaves sourdough bread	2
2 cups	Italian salad dressing of choice	500 mL
8 cups	mixed greens (iceberg lettuce, spinach, romaine)	2 L
1 cup	carrot, shredded	250 mL
1 cup	small zucchini or yellow squash, cut in julienne strips	250 mL
1	English cucumber, peeled and sliced	1
2	avocadoes, seeded, peeled and thinly sliced	2
1	red onion, thinly sliced	1
1 cup	cheese of choice, cubed	250 mL
1 pt	container cherry tomatoes, halved	500 mL
2 cups	seafood of choice, cooked (shrimps, lobster, salmon, halibut, mussels, etc.)	500 mL

Cut 1 inch/2.5 cm slice off top of both loaves of bread. Remove bread from centre of both loaves, leaving shell or bowl about ½ inch/1 cm thick all around. Cut crusts and removed bread into cubes and measure out 4 cups/1 L. Store remainder for future use.

Brush inside of each bread shell with ¼ cup/60 mL dressing. Toss another ¼ cup/60 mL dressing with bread cubes until cubes are well coated. Place bread shells and croutons on baking sheets and bake in preheated 325°F/160°C oven 20 to 25 minutes, until golden; stir croutons around at least once. Cool.

Combine all other ingredients in large salad bowl. Toss with remaining dressing and half of croutons. Divide salad between 2 bread bowls, and top with croutons. Each bowl will serve 2 people. Serve out salad, then break apart sourdough and enjoy with salad.

Serves 4.

Shrimp, Tuna & Orzo Salad

Feta, tuna, shrimp and pasta really work nicely together. This is a 25 minute, special occasion item.

1 cup	orzo pasta	250 mL
¼ cup	olive oil	60 mL
3 tbsp	tarragon vinegar	45 mL
1	garlic clove, minced	1
1 tsp	Dijon mustard	5 mL
¼ tsp	black pepper	1 mL
1 tbsp	fresh dill, chopped	15 mL
1	can (7½ oz/213 g) solid chunk tuna	1
¼ lb	frozen shrimp, thawed	125 g
1	large tomato, seeded and chopped	1
¾ cup	feta cheese, crumbled	180 mL
¼ cup	ripe olives, sliced and pitted	60 mL
¼ cup	green onion, sliced	60 mL

Prepare pasta according to package directions and drain. Mix oil, vinegar, garlic, mustard and pepper in large bowl. Add remaining ingredients, mixing lightly. Refrigerate. Serve on lettuce leaves, if desired.

Serves 2 to 4.

Marinated Lobster

Here's a taste sensation inspired by *Christian's French and Creole Restaurant* in New Orleans. Chef Chris Ansel says you must use taste as your measure, adjusting the amount of herbs according to freshness and strength.

1 lb	lobster meat	500 g
	Fresh mint	
	Salt and cayenne, to taste	
	Brandy	
	Mayonnaise, to taste	

Place lobster, herbs and seasoning in bowl. Sprinkle liberally with brandy and mix well. Cover and let stand several hours or overnight in refrigerator.

When ready to use, add some mayonnaise and mix well. Check seasoning and adjust if necessary. Serve over leaf of curly lettuce and garnish with mint leaf.

Serves 6 to 8 as an appetizer, 4 as a meal.

Shrimp Remoulade Salad

Here is today's variation of a classic French sauce. It's great on a picnic.

¼ cup	prepared mustard	60 mL
1 tsp	horseradish	5 mL
2 tbsp	ketchup	30 mL
¼ tsp	Tabasco sauce	1 mL
½ tsp	salt	2 mL
⅓ cup	beer or ale	80 mL
½ cup	mayonnaise	125 mL
½ cup	green onions, chopped	125 mL
1½ lb	shrimp, cleaned and cooked	750 g
	Salad greens	

Combine first 7 ingredients, beating until well blended. Add green onions and shrimp and let stand 2 to 3 hours in refrigerator, stirring occasionally. Serve on salad greens.

Serves 4 to 6.

Marinated Seafood Bounty

G o wild with your choice of salad greens in this recipe.

½ lb	cooked shrimp, shelled	250 g
½ lb	cooked lobster meat, cut into bite-size pieces (reserve claws for garnish)	250 g
¼ lb	cooked crab meat, flaked	125 g
¼ lb	cooked mussel meats	125 g
	Lemon Vinaigrette (recipe follows)	
2	Roma tomatoes, chopped	2
½ cup	mild sweet onion, chopped	125 mL
6 cups	salad greens, mixed and torn	1.5 L
½ cup	toasted pine nuts	125 mL
	Lemon wedges	

Combine seafood in large bowl and toss with vinaigrette. Marinate several hours or overnight in refrigerator. Remove from refrigerator and allow to warm slightly, then stir in tomatoes and onion. Toss gently with greens and pine nuts. Serve with lemon wedges.

Serves 4.

Lemon Vinaigrette:

1 cup	extra virgin olive oil	250 mL
⅓ cup	lemon juice	80 mL
1 tbsp	lemon zest, grated	15 mL
1	clove garlic, minced	1
1 tbsp	fresh marjoram, chopped	15 mL
1 tbsp	fresh chives, chopped	15 mL
1 tsp	Dijon mustard	5 mL
2 tbsp	capers	30 mL
⅛ tsp	white pepper	0.5 mL
	Salt, to taste (optional)	

Whisk together oil and lemon juice, adding all other ingredients.

Citrus Crab in Savoy Packets

You can present these packets in two ways: cut in half so they look like crab-filled rollups, or in a "package" wrapped in savoy cabbage and tied with a blanched green onion "ribbons."

1	small head of Savoy cabbage	1
½ cup	mayonnaise	125 mL
1	clove garlic, minced	1
2 tsp	fresh tarragon, finely chopped	10 mL
1 cup	cooked crab, shredded	250 mL
2 tbsp	tomato, diced	30 mL
1 tbsp	ketchup	15 mL
2	drops Tabasco sauce	2
1 tsp	bourbon or cognac	5 mL
1	lemon, juice of	1
	Curry Sauce (recipe follows)	
	Yellow and red bell pepper, diced (for garnish)	

Remove outside leaves of cabbage, reserving 8 greenest. Blanch reserved leaves in boiling salted water for 3 minutes. Drain and plunge immediately into bowl of ice water, to stop cooking and set colour. Remove from water, blot on paper towels to dry and set aside. Finely shred centre of cabbage to make 1 cup/250 mL. In large bowl, combine shredded cabbage, mayonnaise, garlic, tarragon, crab, tomatoes, ketchup, Tabasco sauce, bourbon and lemon juice until well mixed. Cover with plastic wrap and place in refrigerator until well chilled.

Remove hard core, or rib, from reserved, blanched cabbage leaves. Using 2 leaves for each serving, on piece of plastic wrap place 1 leaf so that bottom edge overlaps top edge of the other. Make sure there are no spaces open. Spread with ¼ of crab coleslaw, up to ¼ inch/0.5 cm from edge, and roll up like jellyroll. Enclose in plastic wrap and twist ends tightly to compact. Keep refrigerated until ready to use. To serve: cut off ends of each crab roll; then cut in 4 pieces with serrated knife. Stand on end in row in centre of plate. Spoon sauce on each side and garnish with mixed bell peppers.

Serves 2.

Curry Sauce:

¼ cup	mayonnaise	60 mL
6	pinches curry powder	6
2 tbsp	water	30 mL

Mix together ingredients until well blended.

Japanese Noodle Salad with "Hot" Prawns, Red Pepper & Jicama

I particularly like this salad because of the combination of cool (but very tasty) salad combined with warm spicy prawns. The noodle salad can be prepared ahead and then the prawns sautéed and added at the last minute. Jicama is a bulbous root vegetable most likely to be found in a Mexican market. The thin skin should be peeled just before using. If unavailable, substitute water chestnuts. Also, try using different kinds of noodles — buckwheat, rice or wholewheat — to add an interesting texture to the salad. We especially enjoy buckwheat.

For Salad:

¼ cup	Hoisin sauce	60 mL
¼ cup	smooth peanut butter	60 mL
¼ cup	rice vinegar	60 mL
3 tbsp	soy sauce	45 mL
⅓ cup	sesame oil	80 mL
⅛-¼ cup	chili oil (or to taste)	30-60 mL
1	pkg (6 oz/170 g) rice stick (py mai fun)	1
1	pkg (8 oz/227 g) thick Japanese noodles (udon) or other noodles	1
½ lb	jicama (or 1 can water chestnuts)	250 g
1	large red bell pepper, seeded, membranes removed, and cut into julienne strips	1
½ lb	sugar snap peas, thawed if frozen, blanched if fresh	250 g
1 cup	scallions, including most of the green parts, thinly sliced	250 mL
½ cup	chopped peanuts	125 mL

For Shrimp:

2 tbsp	butter	30 mL
1	medium onion, chopped	1
2	cloves garlic, chopped	2
1 tsp	fresh ginger, minced	5 mL
1 lb	shrimp, shelled or in shell, according to preference	500 g
Dash	soy sauce	Dash
Squeeze	lemon juice	Squeeze
	Salt, to taste	
Pinch	cayenne pepper	Pinch
1-2	drops Tabasco sauce	1-2
½ cup	dry white wine	125 mL

Whisk together Hoisin sauce, peanut butter, rice vinegar and soy sauce until smooth. Add sesame and chili oils in slow steady stream, whisking to form emulsion. Set aside.

Fill 2 large pots with water; bring to boil over high heat. Put different noodles in separate pots and cook until tender. Drain well.

Meanwhile, peel and cut jicama into julienne strips. Using large bowl, toss noodles with sauce, mixing well. Add vegetables, scallions and half of peanuts and toss again. Salad can be made the day before, up to this point, and kept refrigerated.

Melt butter in frying pan, and sauté onion, garlic and ginger for 1 to 2 minutes. Add prawns and sauté 5 minutes. Add other ingredients, stirring to deglaze pan and coat shrimp. While shrimp are cooking, divide salad onto serving plates. Add prawns and sprinkle remaining peanuts over all. Serve with Orange Sauce.

Serves 6.

Orange Sauce:

½ cup	light or low-fat sour cream	125 mL
¼ cup	frozen concentrated orange juice, thawed (do not dilute)	60 mL
¼ tsp	horse radish	1 mL
2 oz	Grand Marnier or Orange Liqueur (optional)	60 mL

Combine all ingredients and chill.

Neptune's Nectarine Delight

In the summer when appetites are lighter, salads are a busy cook's mainstay. This one, made with low-fat yogurt and calorie-reduced mayonnaise, is nice and light, allowing the flavours of the sweet nectarines and delicate shrimp to come through.

2 tbsp	plain low-fat yogurt	30 mL
2 tbsp	calorie-reduced mayonnaise	30 mL
2 tbsp	catsup	30 mL
1	clove garlic, finely chopped	1
¼ tsp	pepper	1 mL
2	pinches cayenne pepper	2
1 cup	cooked tiny baby shrimp	250 mL
2	nectarines, diced	2
½ cup	celery, diced	125 mL
½ cup	green onion, thinly sliced	125 mL

Combine first 6 ingredients. Fold in remaining ingredients. Serve on summer greens, or with French bread or sesame buns as a sandwich.

Serves 6.

Summer Harvest Lobster Salad

The yellow and green vegetables of this salad, touched up with red accents from the lobster, add a summery visual image to unusual vegetable combinations. To give this delicious salad a Valentine appeal, use a sharp-tipped paring knife to cut heart shapes from a large red bell pepper. This is easiest when the pepper is whole. Be sure to trim off any seeds from inner membrane.

1	can (11.3 oz/320 g) frozen lobster meat (thawed) *or* meat from 4 small lobster, freshly cooked	1
2 cups	fresh Chinese green beans, cut into 1 inch/2.5 cm pieces	500 mL
2 cups	baby corn on the cob, precooked	500 mL
1	large yellow bell pepper, cut in matchstick strips	1
¼ cup	onion, diced	60 mL
	Small butter lettuce leaves or Belgian endive	
	Lemon wedges	
	Tarragon Dressing (recipe follows)	

Bring medium saucepan of salted water to boil. Add green beans and cook until just tender, about 2 minutes. Drain and transfer to bowl of ice water and cool. Drain beans and corn and place in large bowl with pepper and onion.

Prepare dressing and let stand 1 hour. Meanwhile, separate lobster meat, slicing tails into rounds and checking claws to ensure cartilage has been removed. Divide meat between 4 plates and place on bed of butter lettuce or Belgian endive, with lemon wedge. Reserve 4 claws. (Note: You may wish to set aside smaller pieces of leg or body meat to use later in salad. Or, place under claws and lobster tail medallions.)

To serve, spoon vegetable salad onto plates, using reserved claw to garnish each serving. Remaining dressing should be passed separately.

Serves 4.

Tarragon Dressing:

3 tbsp	tarragon vinegar	45 mL
1 tbsp	cracked black pepper	15 mL
1½ tbsp	coarse-grained mustard	20 mL
1 tbsp	honey	15 mL
¾ cup	vegetable oil	180 mL
3 tbsp	fresh tarragon, finely chopped *or* 2 tsp/10 mL dried tarragon, crumbled	45 mL

Bring vinegar and pepper to simmer in small heavy pan. Whisk in mustard and honey. Gradually whisk in oil. Remove from heat and mix in tarragon. Pour half of dressing over vegetables and let stand at room temperature 1 hour.

Crab Louis

Here's a recipe where simplicity brings tasty results!

1	small to medium-size head iceberg lettuce	1
1½ cups	crab meat, flaked	375 mL
½ cup	mayonnaise	125 mL
¼ cup	chili sauce	60 mL
2 tsp	lime or lemon juice	10 mL
½ tsp	Tabasco sauce	2 mL

Finely shred lettuce; put in salad bowl. Top with crab meat. In small bowl, mix other ingredients and set aside until ready to serve. Just prior to serving, spoon dressing onto salad and toss lightly.

Serves 2.

Mussel & Rice Salad

Steam mussels by placing them in a pot over high heat, covered, until the shells open. Shuck the meat out of all opened mussels and refrigerate until you are ready to make this salad. Mussels are a premier salad ingredient, since they hold their shape and flavour well. They are also reasonably priced.

¼ tsp	saffron powder	1 mL
1 tbsp	mussel liquor	15 mL
1¼ cups	mayonnaise	310 mL
3 cups	saffron-flavoured rice, cooked	750 mL
1½ cups	peas, cooked	375 mL
⅓ cup	parsley, minced	80 mL
2 tbsp	scallions, minced	30 mL
5 lb	cooked mussels	2.5 kg

Mix saffron powder with mussel liquor, then combine with mayonnaise. In salad bowl combine rice, peas, parsley, scallions and mayonnaise mixture. Toss in mussels and chill 3 to 4 hours before serving.

Serves 4 to 6.

Warm Mussel & Potato Salad

There are few dishes that better represent the farming community on my home province of Prince Edward Island than this one. Farmers of the land, who harvest potatoes, and farmers of the sea, who harvest mussels, are equally represented. This recipe does not contain the fat that is usually associated with potato salad made with mayonnaise and eggs.

4 cups	potatoes, diced and boiled	1 L
2 cups	mussel meats	500 mL
2 tbsp	parsley, chopped	30 mL
2 tbsp	green onion tops, minced	30 mL
2 tbsp	green onion whites, minced	30 mL
1 tsp	celery seed	5 mL
½ cup	liquor reserved from steaming clams or bottled clam juice	125 mL
2 tsp	sugar	10 mL
½ cup	white vinegar	125 mL
2 tsp	Dijon mustard	10 mL
	Salt, to taste	
	Red bell pepper or pimento strips, for garnish	

Combine potatoes, mussels, parsley, green onions and celery seed in salad bowl. Combine liquor or clam juice, vinegar, sugar and mustard in saucepan and heat just to boiling. Pour over salad and toss, adding salt if desired. Serve while still warm, garnished with pepper or pimento.

Serves 4.

Creamy Scallop Pasta

Pasta salads have become a North American favourite. This make-ahead delight is ideal for buffets or for enjoying on a hot summer day — or, indeed, anytime at all.

2 cups	rotini pasta, uncooked	500 mL
1 tsp	olive oil	5 mL
1	medium carrot, peeled and cut into julienne strips or matchstick pieces	1
1	stalk celery, cut into julienne strips or matchstick pieces	1
½ cup	squash, cut into julienne strips or matchstick pieces	125 mL
1 tbsp	olive oil	15 mL
1 tsp	fresh lemon juice	5 mL
¼ cup	water	60 mL
	Salt and white pepper, to taste	
1 lb	bay scallops	500 g
1 cup	whipping cream	250 mL
1 tsp	Dijon mustard	5 mL

Cook pasta according to package directions. When done, drain and toss with 1 tsp/5 mL oil.

Sauté vegetables in 1 tbsp/15 mL oil, just until tender but still crunchy. Add lemon juice, water, pepper and salt, to taste. Allow to simmer, covered, 2 to 3 minutes to meld flavours; add scallops. Cover again; simmer 2 to 3 minutes, until scallops are opaque. Remove vegetables and scallops, leaving all stock in pan.

Blend whipping cream and mustard into stock and simmer for 3 to 4 minutes over medium heat to reduce, stirring occasionally. Fold in vegetables and scallops and remove from heat. Stir occasionally while sauce is cooling.

When sauce is lukewarm, toss with pasta and transfer to serving dish. Refrigerate if not serving right away. Should be brought back to room temperature before serving.

Serves 6.

Mandarin Sea Salad

I f you get a chance to make a bulk purchase of halibut, then by all means do so. You may well get a better price for taking a large quantity, halibut freezes well and it is wonderful any way you care to serve it. We often cook more than we need for a meal and then use leftovers in salads like this one.

3 cups	cooked halibut, cut or flaked into chunks	750 mL
¼ cup	mild, sweet onion, finely chopped	60 mL
1 tsp	salt	5 mL
1 cup	celery, thinly sliced	250 mL
1 cup	seedless grapes, halved	250 mL
1	can (10 oz/284 mL) mandarin oranges, drained	1
½ cup	slivered almonds	125 mL
	Salad greens such as lettuce or endive, torn into bite-size pieces	
	Creamy Fish Sauce (recipe follows)	

Combine halibut, onion, salt, celery, grapes and mandarins; chill for several hours. When ready to serve, mix well with torn salad greens and bind with dressing. Garnish with a few mandarins and almonds.

Serves 6.

Creamy Fish Sauce:

2 tbsp	fish stock	30 mL
¼ cup	light cream	60 mL
2 tbsp	mayonnaise	30 mL
½ cup	cooked halibut	125 mL
	Salt and pepper, to taste	

Place all ingredients into electric blender and purée. Season to taste. Serve with salad.

Sardine with Mustard

This salad is a distinctly different addition to a buffet.

3	cans (4¾ oz/133 g each) skinless, boneless sardines, drained	3
1 cup	ripe olives, sliced	250 mL
½ cup	celery, sliced	125 mL
¼ cup	green onions, sliced	60 mL
½ cup	sour cream	125 mL
	Mustard Dressing (recipe follows)	

Combine all ingredients except dressing, tossing well. Chill in refrigerator at least 2 hours before serving. When ready to serve, toss salad in dressing.

Serves 4 to 6.

Mustard Dressing:

1	egg, slightly beaten	1
1 tbsp	butter or margarine	15 mL
¼ cup	vinegar	60 mL
1 tbsp	sugar	15 mL
2 tbsp	prepared mustard	30 mL
½ tsp	paprika	2 mL

Combine all ingredients in small saucepan. Place over low heat and cook, stirring constantly, until slightly thickened. Remove from heat and cool.

Salmon & Bean Salad

Here's an unusual salad with texture, colour and taste to satisfy the senses. It's perfect for a potluck party. To use as a starter course, simply serve smaller portions.

1	can (7 ½ oz/213 g) salmon	1
1	can (19 oz/540 mL) cannellini (white kidney beans)*	1
1	tomato, diced	1
1 cup	celery or green pepper, diced	250 mL
½ cup	fresh parsley, chopped	125 mL
1	clove garlic, minced	1
1	jar (6 oz/170 mL) marinated artichoke hearts, drained and quartered	1
5	black olives, sliced (optional)	5
2 tbsp	wine or white vinegar	30 mL
½ tsp	cumin	2 mL

* Red kidney beans or other cooked or canned white beans may be substituted.

Drain salmon, reserving juices. Place beans in strainer and rinse under cold water; drain well. In salad bowl, combine beans, tomato, celery, parsley, garlic, artichoke hearts, olives, vinegar, cumin and reserved salmon juices. Toss well to mix.

Break salmon into bite-size chunks. Add to salad and toss gently. Serve immediately or refrigerate until needed.

Serves 3.

Kiwi Delight

Some of the best kiwi fruit I have ever tasted came not from New Zealand, but from Canada's west coast. In fact, fellow writer Barb Brennan has a kiwi farm on Vancouver Island and took me on a tour. The kiwi is a fascinating fruit, and a kiwi farm is a fascinating place. If you ever get a chance to visit one, it is well worth the trip. We teamed kiwi with grilled Orange Roughy for a warm salad. It is equally nice if you use leftover halibut or other firm white fish.

3 tbsp	mayonnaise	45 mL
1 tsp	honey	5 mL
1 tsp	prepared mustard	5 mL
¼ tsp	salt (optional)	1 mL
½ cup	celery, diced	125 mL
½ cup	green onion, sliced	125 mL
½ cup	button mushrooms (or larger mushrooms, chopped)	125 mL
¼ cup	yellow bell pepper, finely chopped	60 mL
¼ cup	pine nuts	60 mL
1½ cups	cooked white fish, flaked or cubed	375 mL
1	head butter or iceberg lettuce	1
2	kiwi fruit, peeled and cut into eighths	2

Blend together mayonnaise, honey, mustard and salt. Combine vegetables and nuts with dressing, then gently fold in fish. Don't overwork, or fish will break apart.

Arrange lettuce leaves on 2 serving plates, placing 1 kiwi on each, like petals on a flower. Divide salad and fill centre of plates, so that "petals" are exposed. Sprinkle a few more pine nuts, and a little chopped yellow pepper, over each as garnish.

Serves 2.

Sea Caesar Salad

This salad is delicious served as a light lunch, or as the first course at an elegant dinner party. You can cheat and buy the croutons and dressing, but we are giving you the option of making your own. For a delightful variation from the normal romaine lettuce and mushrooms, we suggest using a head of butter lettuce, a head of red leafed lettuce, a few watercress sprigs and slices of cucumber.

2	slices white bread, cubed	2
1	clove garlic, minced	1
4 tbsp	olive oil	60 mL
1 cup	(or 7½ oz/213 g can) cooked fish of choice (salmon, halibut, haddock, roughy, etc.)	250 mL
1	head romaine lettuce, chopped	1
1½ cups	mushrooms, sliced	375 mL
½ cup	Parmesan cheese, freshly grated	125 mL
	Caesar Salad Dressing (recipe follows, or use commercially prepared dressing)	

Sauté bread with garlic in oil until crisp and golden. Drain on paper towels. Drain fish and flake. Arrange vegetables in salad bowl and top with fish. Spoon on dressing and lightly toss to coat. Sprinkle cheese and croutons over top and serve.

Serves 2 to 4.

Caesar Salad Dressing:

2	egg yolks	2
1 tbsp	Dijon mustard	15 mL
2 tbsp	cider vinegar	30 mL
	Salt and freshly ground black pepper, to taste	
¾ cup	olive oil	180 mL

Place all ingredients except oil in blender or food processor. Blend together and gradually add oil in thick steady stream until thick and creamy.

Delectably Different

International Dishes

*This chapter highlights trendy foods from other lands
and cooking methods a little different from what we are used
to in North America. Most dishes feature ingredients
that can be easily found, although you may have to visit a
specialty food store for some. All the recipes can be
made with the utensils common to most kitchens. Of course,
we have included a few exotic creations that few of you
will cook — but we hope that most of you will enjoy
reading about them.*

Hot & Sour Lobster Soup

V ancouver's Montri Rattanraj, who owns *Montri's*, one of the finest Thai restaurants in Canada, serves authentic Thai cuisine. "Thai cooking," says Montri, "is a careful balancing act of spices, herbs and aromatics. Balancing these flavours and ingredients within each dish and within the meal is critical and is achieved through key ingredients. The three most important are garlic (fragrant); fermented fish sauce (salty); and chilies (hot)." Since living in North America, Montri enjoys lobster in his soups and curries. This and the following recipe from *Montri's* use lobster.

1 tbsp	Thai chili paste	15 mL
3 cups	chicken broth	750 mL
*1	stalk fresh lemon grass (lower ⅓ portion only), cut into 1 inch/2.5 cm sections	1*
2	shallots, sliced	2
*2	keffir lime leaves	2*
*2	slices kha (laos root) (optional)	2*
1 tbsp	bottled fish sauce, to taste (available in Chinese food shops)	15 mL
2 tbsp	lemon juice	30 mL
6	fresh whole red chilies, gently crushed	6
8	canned straw mushrooms, cut in half (optional)	8
¼ lb	lobster meat, cut into bite-size pieces	125 g
1 tbsp	cilantro leaves, chopped, for garnish	15 mL

Combine chili paste and broth in saucepan and bring to boil. Add lemon grass, shallots, lime leaves, kha, fish sauce, lemon juice, chilies and mushrooms; cook gently for 2 minutes. Add lobster and reheat to boiling. Remove from heat and taste for seasonings. To increase saltiness, add fish sauce; to increase sourness, add lemon juice. Pour soup into bowls and garnish with cilantro leaves.

Serves 4.

* Substitutions:

Lemon grass — use 1 tsp/5 mL lemon rind, finely grated, per stalk

Keffir lime leaves — use fresh lemon or lime leaves

Kha — use 4 parts powdered ginger to 1 part powdered cinnamon or cardamom

Montri's Shoo Shee Lobster

2 tbsp	oil	30 mL
2 tbsp	Red Curry Paste (recipe follows)	30 mL
2 cups	coconut milk	500 mL
¼ cup	fish sauce (nam pla)	60 mL
3 tbsp	sugar	45 mL
8-10 oz	lobster meat, large pieces, sliced	250-310 g
5	keffir lime leaves, thinly sliced, for garnish	5
	Steamed rice	

Set wok or skillet over medium-high heat for 30 seconds. Add oil, heat for 30 seconds and add Red Curry Paste. Stir-fry 1 minute and add coconut milk, fish sauce and sugar; heat to boiling. Add lobster and reheat to boiling. Cook about 3 minutes or until lobster is heated through. Transfer to heated platter, garnish with lime leaves and serve immediately with steamed rice.

Serves 4.

Red Curry Paste:

½ cup	onions, chopped	125 mL
8	garlic cloves	8
10	dried red jalapeño chilies	10
4	fresh galangal (a relative of ginger), thinly sliced	4
2 tbsp	lemon grass, chopped	30 mL
1 tbsp	cilantro, chopped	15 mL
1 tsp	cumin	5 mL
1 tsp	shrimp paste	5 mL
1 tsp	salt	5 mL
3 tbsp	oil	45 mL

Combine all ingredients, except oil, in blender and process until smooth. Heat small skillet on medium-high and add oil. Slowly fry curry paste 5 minutes, until fragrant. Remove and store in jar for future use.

Makes 2½ cups/625 mL.

Thai Salmon Noodles

E legant nests of Chinese noodles, topped with oriental tastes and textures, make exquisite appetizers. They can be served as finger food or as a first course, and are a wonderful addition to a celebration of the Chinese New Year. I prefer to buy the best quality red or coho salmon for this recipe. Look for the Chinese-style noodles in the produce section of your grocery store.

1	can (7½ oz/213 g) salmon	1
1	pkg (10½ oz/300 g) Chinese-style noodles	1
1	clove garlic, crushed	1
1 tsp	fresh ginger, chopped	5 mL
1	egg, beaten	1
3 tsp	cornstarch	15 mL
	Oil	
2 tbsp	Hoisin sauce	30 mL
2 tbsp	orange rind	30 mL
1 tbsp	cilantro, chopped	15 mL
	Chili, chopped, for garnish	

Drain salmon, reserving juices. Remove skin and bones, and discard them.

Cook noodles in boiling water and salmon juice for 5 minutes. Drain. Rinse under cold water and drain again thoroughly. Combine noodles, garlic, ginger, egg and 2 tsp/10 mL cornstarch in bowl and mix together well.

Heat oil in frying pan. Drop in ¼ cup/60 mL of noodle mixture. Flatten, shape into a round and cook until noodle cake is deep golden colour on one side. Turn; cook until golden. Drain on paper towels and repeat with remaining mixture, making total of 8 noodle cakes. Keep warm.

Combine Hoisin sauce, 1 tbsp/15 mL orange rind, remaining cornstarch and chopped cilantro in saucepan. Bring to boil, stirring, and simmer for 1 minute or until sauce thickens.

Place 2 noodle cakes on each serving platter. Serve topped with flaked salmon, some sauce, cilantro leaves and sprinkle of orange zest and chopped chili.

Serves 4.

Cantonese Fillets

Ginger root, with its peppery, slightly sweet flavour, has long been a mainstay of oriental cooking. It can be grated, mashed under a cleaver, slivered or even ground. Look for ginger with a smooth skin and a fresh, spicy fragrance. To shred it, peel off the skin and run the ginger through the large openings on a grater. You'll need a bamboo or metal steamer for this recipe. If you have a large bamboo steamer, place it in a wok or skillet to cook. Originally, this method used fish with skin left on; however, we prefer to have the skin removed and place the fillet on lettuce leaves. You can also place a heat-safe plate in the steamer.

2 tbsp	rice wine or sake	30 mL
¼ tsp	salt	1 mL
3	slices ginger root, crushed	3
2 lb	firm-fleshed fish fillets, rinsed and dried	1 kg
2	large lettuce leaves	2
1 tbsp	soy sauce	15 mL
2 tbsp	fish or chicken broth	30 mL
2 tbsp	vegetable oil	30 mL
2 tsp	sesame oil	10 mL
¼ cup	green onion (use white part only), finely sliced	60 mL
1 tbsp	carrot, finely shredded	15 mL
2½ tbsp	ginger root, finely shredded	35 mL
2-3	twists black pepper, freshly ground	2-3

Combine rice wine, salt and ginger root, mashing ginger in liquid. Pour over fillets, turning to coat all sides. Cover and marinate in refrigerator 20 minutes.

Line steamer with lettuce leaves. Place fillets on lettuce. Combine soy sauce and broth and drizzle over fish. Bring water in steaming utensil to full boil; place fish in steam, cover and cook 5 to 12 minutes (depending on thickness and type of fish), until fish flakes.

Combine oils in heavy pan and heat until smoking. Remove fillets to hot serving platter, sprinkle with onion, carrot, shredded ginger root and black pepper; then, slowly pour hot oil over seasonings. Serve immediately.

Serves 6.

Cantonese Apricot & Walnut Fish

This quick and easy entrée takes no more than half an hour to make. Crispy fish is topped with warm apricots and drizzled with zippy apricot sauce.

¾ lb	white fish fillets	375 g
2	eggs	2
2½ tbsp	soy sauce	35 mL
1 cup	walnuts, ground	250 mL
3 tbsp	butter, melted	45 mL
1	can (17 oz/500 mL) apricot halves, reserving syrup	1
2 tbsp	butter	30 mL
1 tbsp	sugar	15 mL
1½ tsp	cornstarch	7 mL
½ tsp	cider vinegar	2 mL
¼ tsp	ground ginger	1 mL
	Parsley, minced	

Cut fish into serving-size portions. Beat eggs with 2 tbsp/30 mL soy sauce. Dip fish in egg mixture, then coat with walnuts. Place in baking dish, drizzle with melted butter and bake at 450°F/230°C for 15 minutes.

Meanwhile, drain apricots, saving syrup. Combine reserved apricot syrup, butter, sugar, cornstarch, vinegar, ginger and remaining ½ tbsp/7 mL soy sauce in saucepan. Cook, stirring over medium-high heat until mixture comes to boil and is thickened. Add apricot halves and heat through.

Arrange baked fish on warmed platter; top with sauce. Garnish with minced parsley. Serve promptly, while fish is crispy.

Serves 4.

Scallop or Lobster Chop Suey

We Canadians love what we call Chinese food. We spend hundreds of dollars a year "ordering in" that which we can easily prepare at home. When my family invites friends over, they often request stir-fry because my spouse is wonderful when it comes to creating culinary treats in the wok. This chop suey is my contribution, along with fried rice, to what is always an enjoyable meal. We usually serve this chop suey with the Crunchy Sesame Shrimp (see next recipe).

2 tbsp	corn oil	30 mL
1	medium onion, cut in wedges	1
2	cloves garlic, minced	2
2 cups	celery, diagonally sliced	500 mL
1 cup	mushrooms, sliced	250 mL
3 cups	bean sprouts	750 mL
¾ lb	small scallops or lobster meat*	375 g
¾ cup	water	180 mL
2 tbsp	corn starch	30 mL
1 tbsp	chicken bouillon concentrate**	15 mL
1 tbsp	soy sauce	15 mL

* If using lobster meat, use 1 can (11.3 oz/213 g), thaw and drain well, and cook enough just to warm.

**Found in the spice department of most stores under the "Bovril" brand name.

If scallops are large, cut into 2 or 3 pieces. In wok or large skillet, heat corn oil over medium-high heat; stir-fry onion and garlic 1 to 2 minutes. Add celery, mushrooms and bean sprouts; stir-fry 1 to 2 minutes. Add scallops or lobster; stir-fry 1 minute.

Mix water, cornstarch, bouillon and soy sauce until smooth; stir into vegetable mixture. Keep stirring constantly while mixture comes to boil; boil 1 minute or until scallops are opaque and sauce has thickened.

Serves 4.

Crunchy Sesame Shrimp with Plum Sauce

The beauty of this and the preceding recipe is that you don't have to visit Chinatown to shop for exotic ingredients. Everything can easily be obtained, and most ingredients are staples we all have in our cupboards.

1 lb	(about 24) large shrimp, shell on	500 g
¾ cup	unsifted all purpose flour	180 mL
¼ cup	cornstarch	60 mL
1 tbsp	baking powder	15 mL
2 tbsp	sesame seeds	30 mL
¼ cup	corn oil	60 mL
¾ cup	cold water	180 mL
	Corn oil, for deep-frying	
	Plum Sauce (recipe follows)	

Shell shrimp, leaving tail section on; devein. Combine flour, cornstarch, baking powder, sesame seeds, corn oil and water. Mix batter until smooth.

Pour corn oil into deep-fryer or large heavy saucepan and heat to 375°F/190°C. Dip shrimp in batter to coat. Slide into hot oil a few at a time and deep-fry 1 to 2 minutes, or until golden brown. Drain on paper towels and keep warm in oven until all are cooked. Serve with plum sauce on side.

Serves 4.

Plum Sauce:

1	can (14 oz/398 mL) pitted purple plums, drained	1
½ cup	golden corn syrup	125 mL
¼ cup	lemon juice	60 mL
¼ cup	soy sauce	60 mL
½ tsp	ground ginger	2 mL

Place all ingredients in blender and cover. Blend on high speed until smooth (about 30 seconds). Pour into small saucepan and cook over medium heat, stirring occasionally, for about 10 minutes. Serve as dipping sauce.

Bangladeshi Fish in Sauce

Immensely popular in its home country, this dish is usually served with steamed rice.

1½ lb	haddock, cod or other firm-fleshed, white fish, cut into 2 inch/5 cm cubes	750 g
1 tsp	salt	5 mL
1½ tsp	ground turmeric	7 mL
	Vegetable oil	
1 tbsp	ground coriander	15 mL
1½ tsp	fresh ginger, finely grated	7 mL
1 tsp	cumin	5 mL
½ tsp	chili powder	2 mL
4	whole red chilies	4
2	bay leaves	2
1	large onion, peeled and chopped	1
1	clove garlic, chopped	1

Rub fish with ½ tsp/2 mL salt and ½ tsp/2 mL turmeric. Set aside 15 minutes. Then, heat oil in skillet and brown fish pieces lightly. Lift out fish with slotted spoon.

Mix ground coriander, ginger, cumin, chili powder, remaining turmeric and remaining salt with 3 tbsp/45 mL water. Remove most of oil from skillet and heat about 5 tbsp/75 mL water over medium heat. Add red chilies and bay leaves. As chilies and bay leaves darken, add onion and garlic and fry until golden brown. Add spice mixture; stir and fry 1 minute. Then add fish pieces and 1 cup water. Spread pieces evenly around bottom of pan and lay chilies on top. Simmer 2 to 3 minutes, spooning sauce over fish.

Cover pan and leave on low heat about 15 minutes, until fish is done. Serve with plain rice.

Serves 6.

Caribbean Baked Red Snapper

This whole baked red snapper is from *Victor's Cafe 52* in Miami. Victor del Corral was featured in *Restaurants and Institutions* magazine for his sensational seafood dishes from the Caribbean. Baked whole fish is common in Cuban cuisine. Be sure you have a baking dish big enough — I used a throw-away turkey pan. For an authentic presentation, take the fish to the table whole.

1 cup	olive oil	250 mL
1 tbsp	sweet paprika	15 mL
1	garlic head, peeled and finely chopped	1
1 tsp	oregano	5 mL
¼ cup	white wine	60 mL
3 tbsp	Seville orange juice	45 mL
	or mixture of equal parts orange and lime juices	
2 tsp	salt	10 mL
1 tsp	white pepper	5 mL
1	(8 lb/4 kg) whole red snapper, cleaned and scaled	1
4	large potatoes, pared and thinly sliced	4
¼ cup	olive oil	60 mL
3	large red bell peppers, seeded, cut in thick diagonal slices	3
3	large onions, pared, cut in thick diagonal slices	3
	Cherry tomatoes	
	Fresh parsley or other herb, for garnish	

Combine 1 cup/250 mL oil, paprika, garlic, oregano, wine, orange juice, salt and pepper; mix well. Rub mixture inside fish and all over fish surface. Allow fish to rest in marinade at least 1 hour before cooking.

Smother sliced potatoes with ¼ cup/60 mL olive oil; arrange on baking dish to provide bed for snapper. Cover potatoes with layer of red peppers and onions. Sprinkle with additional olive oil. Place fish over vegetables. Bake at 350°F/180°C for 1 hour, until its flesh looks white and opaque when flaked with fork. Serve morsels of fish garnished with cherry tomato and parsley and accompanied by baked vegetables and simple avocado salad.

Serves 6 to 8.

Cuban Stew

This seafood stew is reminiscent of those to be had in Cuba, where it would be served with a Cuban beer and crusty bread to soak up the juices. To give an authenticity to the dish, use six allspice berries in place of the ground allspice. Crack them by crushing them with a mortar or under a wide blade knife. Be sure to do as the Cubans do — vary the fish according to what is fresh at your seafood market.

1	2x4-inch/5x10-cm piece salt pork (if watching fat, use 2 tbsp/30 mL safflower oil instead)	1
2	onions, chopped	2
4	cloves garlic, crushed	4
3	stalks celery, chopped	3
1	red bell pepper	1
3	jalapeño peppers*, seeded and chopped	3
½	bay leaf	½
4 cups	fish stock (or use chicken)	1 L
¼ tsp	ground allspice	1 mL
1 tsp	crushed red pepper*	5 mL
1 lb	red snapper fillets, cut into 2 inch/5 cm pieces	500 g
1 cup	fresh spinach, shredded	250 mL
	Cilantro, chopped	
	Lime wedges	

* If you like food that sizzles with heat, increase the amount of jalapeño and crushed red pepper, to taste.

Heat salt pork, or safflower oil, in large stew pot until bubbling. Sauté next 5 ingredients until softened. If salt pork is used, remove. Add bay leaf, stock, allspice and red pepper. Simmer 15 minutes. Add fish; simmer further 5 minutes.

To serve, ladle into large soup bowls; top each with shredded spinach and cilantro and serve immediately with wedges of lime for squeezing into soup.

Serves 6.

Brazilian Vatapa with Palm Hearts

Vatapa is one of Brazil's most loved dishes. This recipe comes from Joyce Goldstein, owner of San Francisco's *Square One* restaurant, who went to Brazil to research vatapa and other traditional dishes. To come as close to duplicating her version as possible, you should make the shrimp stock. However, if you wish to save yourself some work, you can use fish or chicken stock.

½ cup	ginger root, peeled and sliced	125 mL
1 tbsp	paprika	15 mL
2 tbsp	lemon juice	30 mL
6 tbsp	mild olive oil	90 mL
3	large yellow onions (about 6 cups/1.5 L), diced	3
6	cloves garlic, finely minced	6
3	hot peppers, finely minced (or cayenne to taste)	3
3 cups	canned plum tomatoes, diced	750 mL
½ cup	reserved juice from canned tomatoes	125 mL
½ cup	coconut cream (or more, to taste — canned is fine)	125 mL
½ cup	dry roasted peanuts or cashews or both, finely ground	125 mL
½ cup	toasted unsweetened coconut, pulsed in processor	125 mL
4 tbsp	cilantro, chopped	60 mL
5 cups	stock (shrimp is best, but fish or chicken will do)*	1.25 L
2 lb	prawns or very large shrimp, shelled and deveined (save shells)	1 kg
1 lb	rockfish, flounder, snapper or sea bass cut into 1x3 inch/2.5x7.5 cm strips	500 g
	Salt and freshly ground pepper, to taste	
	Rice, cooked	
	Deep Fried Palm Hearts (recipe follows)	
	Additional coarsely chopped nuts, coconut and cilantro, for garnish	

* **To make stock:** Heat a little olive oil in large pot; add shells and stir 1 minute. Add chopped onion, piece of celery, a few peppercorns, bay leaf and sprig of cilantro; cover with 5 cups water/1.25 L. Bring to boil, turn heat down very low and simmer 1 hour. Strain to use. Should make about 4 cups/1 L stock, after evaporation.

Place ginger root in blender or food processor and purée with paprika and lemon juice. Heat 3 tbsp/45 mL oil in large saucepan. Add onions and cook over low heat until tender. Add puréed ginger mixture, garlic and hot peppers. Cook for a few minutes. Add half of tomatoes, their liquid and coconut cream and cook for a few minutes. Add nuts, toasted coconut and half of chopped cilantro and cook for a few minutes more. Purée sauce in blender or processor.

Return puréed mixture to saucepan and add rest of diced tomatoes, stock, and remaining cilantro. Bring up to slow simmer and cook about 10 minutes until sauce is rich and somewhat thick.

Take fish and shrimp from refrigerator. Sprinkle with salt and pepper. Heat remaining oil in skillet and sauté fish and prawns over high heat. Add prepared sauce. Heat through.

Serve over rice with palm hearts (recipe follows) on side. Garnish with additional chopped nuts, coconut and cilantro.

Serves 6.

Deep Fried Palm Hearts:

1	can (14 oz/398 mL) palm hearts	1
2	eggs, lightly beaten	2
	Salt and pepper, to taste	
	Breadcrumbs	
	Oil, for frying	

Drain palm hearts and cut each one in half (you need enough pieces for 6 plates). Mix eggs with seasonings. Roll palm hearts in eggs, then in breadcrumbs. Deep-fry in deep fat at 375°F/190°C.

Mexican Camarones en Chileajo

(Spicy Shrimp with Red Chili)

Chef Rick Bayless of the *Frontera Grill* in Chicago claims that this dish comes straight from Oaxaca in southern Mexico. This Mexican restaurant specializes in authentic regional Mexican food, which Bayless says is vastly different from the American style or Southwest Cookery that we commonly think of as "Mexican." He travelled thousands of miles in Mexico before opening the restaurant. This shrimp dish is just a sample of what he found.

16	medium dried chilies guajillos, stemmed, seeded and deveined	16
	Boiling water	
12	garlic cloves, unpeeled	12
½ tsp	black peppercorns	2 mL
8	cloves	8
2 tsp	oregano (Mexican is preferable)	10 mL
3½ cups	fish broth	875 mL
8 tbsp	olive oil	120 mL
2 tbsp	cider vinegar	30 mL
2-3 tsp	sugar	10-15 mL
	Salt, to taste	
48	shrimp, medium large	48
3	plantains, ripe, sliced diagonally ¼ inch/0.5 cm thick	3
1 cup	frozen peas, defrosted	250 mL
	Flat-leaf parsley, for garnish	

Tear chilies into flat pieces; toast a few at a time on griddle or heavy skillet over medium heat. Press firmly with spatula until chilies crackle, blister and change colour. Turn; repeat. Remove from griddle to bowl. In bowl, cover chilies with boiling water. Weight with plate to keep submerged. Soak 20 minutes.

Meanwhile, cook garlic on griddle or skillet over medium heat, turning frequently, until charred in spots and soft — about 15 minutes. Drain chilies; discard water. Place chilies and garlic in blender jar; reserve.

Grind peppercorns and cloves in mortar; add to chili mixture in jar. Add oregano and 2 cups/500 mL fish broth; blend until smooth. Strain through medium-mesh sieve. Heat 2 tbsp/30 mL olive oil in large saucepan over high heat. When quite hot, add chili mixture; stir until darker and thicker, about 4 to 5 minutes. Add vinegar and enough fish broth to give consistency of heavy cream. Partially cover; simmer over medium-low heat 30 minutes. Add sugar; season with salt, to taste. Toss shrimp with 1 tbsp/15 mL sauce to coat, and set aside.

Heat 2 tbsp/30 mL olive oil in large, non-stick skillet over medium heat. Fry plantain slices in batches, adding oil to skillet as necessary, until browned — 3 to 5 minutes per side. Remove to baking sheet; keep warm in low oven. Add oil to skillet, if necessary. Fry shrimp in batches until just done, 2 to 4 minutes per side. Keep warm in low oven. Warm peas in small saucepan. To serve, ladle sauce to barely cover centres of 6 warm dinner plates. Arrange shrimp and plantains around outside of plates. Garnish with peas and parsley leaves.

Serves 6.

Mejillónes con Salsa de Almendras

(Spanish Mussels with Almond Sauce)

This easy-to-prepare appetizer will bring a touch of Spain to your table.

24	large mussels, cleaned and steamed	24
24	blanched, toasted almonds	24
1	slice white bread	1
½ cup	olive oil	125 mL
1 tbsp	red-wine vinegar	15 mL
Dash	Tabasco sauce	Dash
	Salt and pepper, to taste	

Remove meat from mussels. Combine rest of ingredients in food processor until smooth. Place mussel meats on serving dish, spoon sauce over mussels and chill, covered, for 1 hour before serving.

Serves 4 as a first course.

Italian Cioppino

The Italians have many ways of preparing mussels, the most delightful of which — to my mind at least — is to combine them with fish and other shellfish in a tomato sauce that is absolutely delicious when soaked up with crusty bread at the meal's finale. I usually use a rich vegetable pasta sauce for the tomato sauce that is called for here. Vary the seafood according to availability and serve this to a group who will enjoy a nourishing, hot and immensely satisfying meal. The sauce can be made ahead and the seafood prepared so that all you have to do is simmer it together at the last minute. In fact, I often double the sauce recipe (because I tend to get carried away and add more than listed) — use enough to cook the seafood and freeze the rest for future use.

⅔ cup	onion, chopped	160 mL
½ cup	green pepper, chopped	125 mL
½ cup	celery, chopped	125 mL
¼ cup	carrot, chopped	60 mL
2 tbsp	olive oil	30 mL
1	large garlic clove, minced	1
1	can (35 oz/1 L) Italian plum tomatoes	1
½ cup	tomato sauce	125 mL
1 tsp	basil	5 mL
½ tsp	oregano	2 mL
1	bay leaf	1
	Salt and pepper, to taste	
¾ cup	dry white wine	180 mL
16	mussels, cleaned	16
16	soft-shell clams	16
½ lb	halibut, haddock or swordfish*, skinned and cut into 8 or more chunks	250 g
8	shrimp, shelled and deveined	8
8	scallops (cut any very large ones in half)	8
1	cooked lobster, chopped into 8 pieces	1

* Sometimes it is more economical to buy "chowder" mix — small pieces of a variety of fish.

In large soup kettle or saucepan, sauté onion, pepper, celery and carrot in olive oil over medium-high heat for 3 minutes, stirring twice. Add garlic and cook until vegetables are softened. Add tomatoes (including juice), sauce, basil, oregano, bay leaf, and salt and pepper, to taste. Simmer, covered, for 1 hour, stirring occasionally. At this stage you can refrigerate the sauce for later use.

When almost ready to serve meal (table should be set), add wine to sauce and bring mixture to boil over medium-high heat. Add mussels and clams; cook, covered, for 3 minutes. Add fish, shrimp and scallops; simmer, covered, for 3 to 5 minutes until shellfish are open and fish cooked. Add lobster. Discard any unopened shellfish, and bay leaf. To serve, ladle into heated bowls, making sure that everyone gets 1 piece of each seafood. Garnish by sprinkling with chopped cilantro. Serve with chunks of crusty bread for complete meal.

Serves 4 to 6.

Scampi

Scampi is the Italian name for the tail portion of any of several varieties of lobsterettes or prawns. In North America, scampi often describes very large shrimp that are split, brushed with garlic oil or butter and broiled. We've added a modern touch and microwaved them!

2	large cloves garlic, minced	2
1 tbsp	olive oil	15 mL
1 lb	large to extra-large shell-on shrimp, peeled and deveined	500 g
2 tbsp	fresh parsley, chopped	30 mL
	Juice of ½ lemon	
	Salt and pepper, to taste	

In large microwave dish, cook garlic in oil on high 1 minute. Add shrimp in single layer, cover with plastic wrap and microwave on high 1 minute. Turn dish and cook additional 1½ minutes. Let stand 2 minutes.

Uncover. Add parsley and lemon juice; season to taste. Toss to blend flavours.

Serves 4.

Salmon Tartare

The term "tartare" probably originated in the Baltic Provinces of what used to be Russia, where, in medieval times, the Tartars shredded red meat with a knife and ate it raw. In modern times, it has come to signify raw meat and can be applied to seafood as well as the traditional beef. You should buy top-quality salmon for this recipe. Be sure that it has been previously frozen — this arrests any bacterial growth that may irritate the stomach. This recipe comes from the west coast of Canada, where oriental cuisine from many cultures is very much enjoyed.

1 lb	boneless salmon fillets, chopped small	500 g
2 tbsp	capers	30 mL
2 tbsp	red onion	30 mL
½ oz	anchovy	15 g
4	slices rye bread, toasted	4
4	egg yolks	4
	Salt and pepper, to taste	
Pinch	nutmeg	Pinch
Dash	Worcestershire sauce	Dash

There are 2 ways to serve this dish. The first is to place all ingredients individually on platters or serving plates and allow people to serve their own (chop onion and capers separately).

The second method is as follows: Chop capers, onion and anchovy together until all are finely minced. In mixing bowl, knead salmon and minced mixture together until texture is consistent. Season with salt, pepper and Worcestershire sauce, to taste. Form into 4 square patties and place on toasted rye rounds. Separate egg yolks, placing yolk into half of shell and positioning in centre of each salmon patty. Garnish with onion slices and capers.

Serves 4 to 8.

Pacific Halibut with Black Butter & White Endive Salad

H ere is an updated version of the classic French "beurre noir."

4	(about 6 oz/185 g each) halibut steaks	4
2 tbsp	flour	30 mL
	Salt and pepper, to taste	
5 tbsp	butter	75 mL
1 tbsp	lemon juice	15 mL
2 tbsp	fresh parsley, chopped	30 mL
	White Endive Salad (recipe follows)	

Sprinkle halibut with flour seasoned with salt and pepper. In heavy skillet, melt 2 tbsp/30 mL butter. Add halibut and sauté over medium-high heat about 5 minutes each side or until fish is opaque and flakes when fork-tested. Remove halibut to heated platter or serving plates.

Add remaining butter to skillet; heat until butter turns light brown. Immediately remove skillet from heat. Stir in lemon juice and parsley; pour over halibut and serve with White Endive Salad.

Serves 4.

White Endive Salad:
I've always known these tightly folded cigar-shaped little vegetables as "Belgian endive." The creamy leaves with pale yellow tips have a crisp texture and delicately bitter flavour. To prepare them, remove outer leaves, cut off the bottom and slice. You may want to remove the centre core, as it can be bitter.

1 lb	white endives, sliced across	500 g
2	medium apples, diced with peel on	2
1 cup	fresh or canned mandarin oranges	250 mL
⅓ cup	vinaigrette or Italian dressing	80 mL
2 tbsp	orange juice	30 mL
	Cilantro or parsley, chopped, for garnish	

Toss ingredients together. Refrigerate before serving.

Serves 4 to 6.

Seattle Scallops in White Wine, Shallots & Herbs

The cuisine of the Pacific Northwest has come into its own in the early '90s. Any seafood lover will appreciate a visit to the coastal areas of Washington State and British Columbia, where one can seek out the trendsetting chefs and restaurateurs. Chef Wayne Ludvigsen of the renowned *Ray's Boathouse* in Seattle is noted for transforming the former fish-and-chip restaurant into a full-service fresh seafood restaurant. He joined the staff at sixteen as a summer employee and rose to the position of head chef, learning several lifetimes' worth of truths about fish along the way. He tends to keep preparations simple and the product first-rate. This recipe also works with mussels.

1 lb	unshelled pink or bay scallops or mussels	500 g
¼ cup	white wine	60 mL
4 tbsp	butter	60 mL
1	shallot, chopped	1
Pinch	thyme	Pinch
1	broken bay leaf	1
	Black pepper, freshly ground, to taste	

Scrub scallop or mussel shells clean. In large saucepan, bring wine, butter, shallot, thyme, bay leaf and pepper to boil.

Add shellfish, cover tightly and steam over low heat until scallops are just cooked through and begin to fall from shells, 2 to 3 minutes. If using mussels, cook just until open, about 5 to 10 minutes.

Discard bay leaf from broth. Serve shellfish in broth, in warm bowls.

Serves 4.

Santa Fe Crab & Sea Scallop Cakes

Somehow we don't associate seafood with New Mexico. Instead, we have visions of cuisine featuring longhorn steak, cactus leaves and salsa. The *Santa Cafe* in Santa Fe set out to prove that vision wrong, with these delightful cakes. They are hot to the northern palette, so I suggest serving with a cool, crisp salad.

2 cups	scallops, coarsely chopped	500 mL
1 lb	lump crab meat, picked free of cartilage and shell	500 g
2 tsp	Dijon mustard	10 mL
2 tbsp	mayonnaise	30 mL
3 tbsp	red onion, chopped	45 mL
2 tsp	garlic, finely minced	10 mL
1	egg	1
1 tsp	salt	5 mL
1 tsp	pepper	5 mL
2 tbsp	cilantro, chopped	30 mL
	Juice of 1 lemon	
10	dashes Tabasco sauce	10
1 cup	breadcrumbs	250 mL
½ cup	sweet butter, softened	125 mL

Combine all ingredients in medium-size bowl. Form mixture into individual ¼ cup/60 mL crab cakes.

Heat non-aluminum sauté pan. Melt 1 tbsp/15 mL butter in preheated pan. Sauté individual cakes until golden brown — about 4 minutes per side.

Serves 4 to 6.

Caribbean Crunchy Coconut Prawns

Think exotic fruits, fresh seafood, coconut and hot peppers in any form, and you have Caribbean food. For a quick tropical fix, serve these coconut prawns with rice, a tangy salad and exotic vegetables as a dinner or with the Hot Citrus Dipping Sauce as an appetizer. Combine with some exotic rum drinks, a limbo stick and the sound of reggae and you have an at-home Caribbean escape from winter.

1	egg yolk	1
1⅓ cups	ice water	330 mL
1 cup	all purpose flour	250 mL
1 cup	unsweetened shredded coconut	250 mL
	Vegetable oil, for deep-frying	
1½ lb	medium, uncooked prawns or large shrimp, peeled and deveined	750 g
	Hot Citrus Dipping Sauce (recipe follows)	

Prepare batter by beating egg yolk lightly with whisk, slowly adding water, beating constantly and then mixing in flour and ½ cup/125 mL coconut. Do not overbeat. Place batter in refrigerator to chill at least 30 minutes.

Prepare oil for deep-frying, either in deep-fryer, or by pouring at least 2 inches/5 cm in deep, heavy saucepan. Roll prawns in remaining coconut, dip in batter and gently shake off excess. When oil is 375°F/190°C, add prawns a few at a time and cook, turning once, until golden brown. Remove, drain and place on paper towels.

Keep cooked prawns warm in 200°F/100°C oven until all are cooked and then serve immediately with dipping sauce.

Serves 6 as a main course, 12 as an appetizer.

Hot Citrus Dipping Sauce:

⅓ cup	sugar	80 mL
1 tsp	cornstarch	5 mL
⅓ cup	boiling water	80 mL
1 tbsp	jalapeño pepper, finely minced	15 mL
2 tbsp	lemon or lime juice	30 mL
1 tbsp	orange peel, finely grated	15 mL

In small saucepan combine sugar and cornstarch, add boiling water and bring to boil. Lower heat and simmer, stirring occasionally, until mixture begins to thicken. Remove from heat and cool to room temperature. Stir in pepper, juice and grated peel and place in serving bowl, then garnish with zest of orange.

Louisiana Oysters Casino

3	slices of bacon, roughly chopped	3
¼ cup	onion, chopped	60 mL
¼ cup	green pepper, chopped	60 mL
2 tbsp	celery, chopped	30 mL
1 tsp	lemon juice	5 mL
½ tsp	salt	2 mL
¼ tsp	Tabasco sauce	1 mL
½ tsp	Worcestershire sauce	2 mL
1 pt	oysters, drained	500 mL
	Lemon wedges and fresh herbs, for garnish	

Fry bacon in skillet. Add onion, pepper, celery; cook until tender. Stir in lemon juice, salt, Tabasco and Worcestershire sauce. Place oysters in shallow, buttered baking dish. Spread bacon mixture over oysters. Bake in 400°F/200°C oven for 10 minutes, until edges of oysters begin to curl. Garnish with lemon wedges and fresh herbs, if desired.

Serves 6.

Crawfish Jambalaya

A trip to New Orleans turned into one of our most enjoyable travel experiences ever. We were attending a conference hosted by the International Association of Culinary Professionals, and, as you would imagine, ate up a storm! Never a day passed that we didn't stroll into the French Quarter to sample yet another example of wonderful cuisine. Happily, our trip coincided with the months when crawfish are the most plentiful. We ate them in every way possible, including at gourmet breakfasts and a "boil up" beside the Mississippi. It isn't easy to duplicate Louisiana recipes because of their abundant supply of spices and specialized ingredients such as crawfish fat, which is used as a flavouring in many crawfish dishes. These recipes are adaptations, but still delicious. If you can, use a smoked sausage. If crawfish is not available, substitute lobster meat.

1 lb	sausage, sliced	500 g
1 cup	bell pepper, chopped	250 mL
1 cup	celery, chopped	250 mL
1 cup	onion, chopped	250 mL
½ cup	green onions, chopped	125 mL
2	cloves garlic, minced	2
1 cup	rice, uncooked	250 mL
2 cups	water	500 mL
1	can (16 oz/455 g) tomatoes	1
½ cup	stewed tomatoes	125 mL
1 lb	crawfish tails	500 g
2 tsp	creole seasoning* or salt and pepper, to taste	10 mL
1 tsp	hot sauce	5 mL

* Look for this seasoning in the spice section of your food store.

Sauté sausage, bell peppers, celery, onions, and garlic in large, deep skillet. Cook until tender but not brown. Stir in remaining ingredients. Bring to boil. Stir once or twice and reduce heat. Cover and simmer 20 minutes, or until rice is tender. Mixture should be slightly moist. Adjust seasonings to taste. Fluff with fork and serve.

Serves 10.

Creole Lobster (or Crawfish)

If you are making this down south, shelled crawfish is used instead of lobster. In Canada and the northern states, lobster is more readily available. A similar stew, called enchilado, is made in Cuba using rock lobster tails and crab. If you want a very showy presentation, use lobster tails cut across to make fairly thick medallions. Otherwise, do as we do and use the tails and claws from frozen canned lobster meat (reserving the broken and body meat for a salad or sandwiches the next day). Serve over white rice with a crisp green salad.

¼ cup	olive oil	60 mL
4	cloves garlic, minced	4
1	medium onion, finely chopped	1
1	large yellow bell pepper, seeded and finely chopped	1
1	jalapeño pepper, seeded and finely chopped (optional)	1
3 tbsp	fresh cilantro or Italian parsley, finely chopped	45 mL
	or 1 tbsp/15 mL dried cilantro or Italian parsley	
1	bay leaf	1
1 tsp	oregano	5 mL
¼ tsp	thyme	1 mL
2 cups	tomato sauce	500 mL
1 cup	beer	250 mL
2 tsp	salt, or less to taste	10 mL
4 cups	cooked lobster meat	1 L
	White rice, cooked	

Heat oil and sauté garlic until lightly browned. Add onion, peppers, parsley, bay leaf, oregano and thyme. Cook 3 minutes then pour in tomato sauce and beer and add salt. Stir to combine ingredients.

Simmer over medium heat 10 minutes or until sauce thickens slightly, stirring occasionally. Add lobster and continue cooking 3 to 4 minutes, until heated through. Serve immediately over white rice.

Serves 8.

Sooke Harbour House

O ne of the most innovative seafood chefs in North American lives on Vancouver Island, off the western coast of British Columbia. This is Sinclair Philip who, along with his wife Fredrica, operates Sooke Harbour House, a restaurant and inn on Whiffen Spit Road in Sooke. If you have a yen for the unusual and wish to sample exotic foods prepared in an exotic setting by masters of their craft, and if you also have an appreciation for freshness and natural flavour, then make the effort to enjoy their hospitality.

The dishes that follow are not ones you are likely to make yourself, simply because the ingredients are not readily available. I have included them to give you the pleasure of reading how true experts prepare things that most of us have never heard of or seen. It should also be noted that many of these shellfish are now protected, with harvesting very closely regulated — the opportunities to enjoy them are few and far between.

Oysters with Carrot Sauce

T his dish is by Chef Gordon Cowen, who notes that an excellent substitute in this recipe is to use butternut squash instead of carrots, or to combine the two.

½	small onion, very thinly sliced	½
2	cloves garlic, finely chopped	2
4 tbsp	unsalted butter	60 mL
2	medium-size carrots (young tops are preferred), very thinly sliced	2
¼ cup	well-reduced fish stock	60 mL
1 oz	Vermouth or dandelion wine	30 mL
2 tbsp	lemon juice	30 mL
12	large Pacific or Golden Mantle oysters	12

Sauté onions and garlic in 2 tbsp/30 mL butter. Add carrots and fish stock and cook covered over low heat until carrots are tender. Purée mixture in blender or food processor. Add Vermouth and lemon juice and whisk in remaining butter. Adjust seasoning and thickness, to taste.

Place sauce on 4 plates with 3 grilled or sautéed oysters on each and garnish with something green, such as wild Siberian miners' lettuce or broad-leaf Italian parsley.

Serves 4.

Sea Urchin Soup

One seafood that is not endangered is the sea urchin. For years North Americans ignored this prickly little sea dweller, but when the Japanese began to buy up the roe, chefs like Sinclair Philip tuned into this delicacy. This recipe was created by Chef Ron Cherry of *Sooke Harbour House*. He says to use only fresh sea urchin, rather than canned or preserved, in this dish.

1	medium-size, fresh sea urchin (approximately 2½ oz/75 mL roe)	1
2 tbsp	unsalted butter	30 mL
1-2	shallots, finely minced	1-2
3 oz	dry Gewurztraminer (or substitute dry pear cider)	90 mL
¼ cup	fish stock	60 mL
¼ cup	whipping cream	60 mL
8	1-inch/2.5-cm long chives	8
1	2-inch/5-cm square freshly harvested sea lettuce, rinsed in several quick changes of fresh water, torn into small pieces (optional)	1
1	large leaf red shiso (optional)	1

To clean sea urchin: With sharp knife, cut through test (spiny shell) of sea urchin to open shell. Remove 5 orange-yellow roe sacs and clean away clinging viscera (anything that is not yellow or orange roe). Discard viscera and test. Purée 4 roe sacks in small blender (makes about 2 oz/60 mL). Reserve remaining roe sack, intact, for garnish. Set aside.

Place medium-size saucepan on medium-low heat. Coat bottom with 1 tbsp/15 mL butter and add shallots. When shallots begin to sweat (about 2 minutes), add 2 oz/60 mL wine. Bring to boil and boil 1 minute over medium-high heat to reduce wine. Add fish stock and whipping cream. Whisk well and cook over medium heat 5 minutes. Whisk soup again. Remove pan from heat and add puréed sea urchin row and 1 oz/30 mL wine. Whisk thoroughly. Do not cook roe on stove or it will lose fruitiness and develop egg-like flavour.

To prepare garnish, warm frying pan over low heat. Coat bottom with 1 tbsp/15 mL butter and add sea lettuce and intact urchin roe sack. Stir and let warm gently over low heat approximately 30 seconds, until warmed through. Ladle soup carefully into large, white soup bowl. Place warmed sea lettuce and roe artfully in centre. Garnish with chives and shiso leaf. Serve immediately.

Serves 1.

Crab Acapulco

I have a passion for the combination of avocado and seafoods such as crab and lobster. My passion originated in England, where we were served a delightful crab and prawn cocktail in a halved avocado — I was hooked! The idea of serving the avocados warm, as in this dish, intrigued me, and once I tried it I was hooked once again. Use fruit that is free of bruises or gouges and yields to pressure from your hand when gently squeezed. Serve nestled in rice, with crisp asparagus alongside.

¼ cup	butter or margarine	60 mL
¼ cup	sifted all purpose flour	60 mL
1⅔ cups	milk	410 mL
¾ tsp	salt	3 mL
1 tsp	Worcestershire sauce	5 mL
Dash	(generous) cayenne pepper	Dash
2 tbsp	fresh lime (or lemon) juice	30 mL
3 tbsp	sherry	45 mL
⅓ cup	sharp Cheddar cheese, grated	80 mL
2 cups	cooked crab meat, picked clean of shell and cartilage	500 mL
4	avocados	4
	Salt	
	Toasted coconut *or* toasted sesame seeds	

Melt butter and blend in flour. Gradually mix in milk and cook and stir until smooth and thickened. Add salt, Worcestershire sauce, cayenne, lime juice, sherry and cheese, stirring until blended. Add crab meat and cook just until heated.

Cut avocados in half; remove seed and skin. Place in shallow baking dish; sprinkle with salt. Heap each avocado half with crab mixture and sprinkle of toasted coconut.

Bake in slow oven 300°F/150°C for 15 minutes, just until warm. Do not bake longer.

Serves 8 as an appetizer, or 4 as a main course.

Spanish Paella

This dish of saffron-flavoured rice is named after the special two-handled pan in which it is traditionally prepared and served.

8	mussels, scrubbed clean	8
8	clams, brushed free of sand	8
	Black pepper, to taste	
1	chicken (approximately 2 lb/1 kg), cut into serving pieces and skinned	1
¼ cup	corn oil	60 mL
2	garlic cloves, coarsely chopped	2
1	onion, chopped	1
1	red pepper, seeded, minced	1
2	squid, drained, washed and chopped (optional)	2
2 tsp	paprika	10 mL
1 cup	fresh peas	250 mL
2 cups	long or short grain rice, cooked	500 mL
4 cups	chicken broth	1 L
¼ tsp	saffron threads, softened in small bowl of water *or* ½ tsp/2 mL powdered saffron	1 mL
4 oz	lobster meat (1 lobster), chopped	125 g
3 oz	shrimp, cooked	90 g
	Lemon wedges	

Cook mussels and clams in boiling water for 5 minutes. Throw out any unopened shells. Set aside. Sprinkle chicken pieces with pepper. In paella dish or casserole, heat oil and fry chicken until golden. Add garlic, onion, red pepper and squid. Stir well and fry until onion is tender. Sprinkle with paprika. Add peas and rice; cook, stirring frequently, until rice is lightly golden.

In casserole dish, bring chicken broth to boil and pour over rice mixture along with saffron. Stir well and cook over high heat for about 5 minutes. Add mussels, clams, lobster and shrimp. Reduce heat, cover and simmer 10 minutes, without stirring. Set aside 5 minutes. Serve in casserole, garnished with lemon wedges.

Serves 4.

Index

About the Author

Julie V. Watson is a widely published
food writer. Her previous books include *Seafood
Cookery of Prince Edward Island, Largely Lobster,
Barbecuing Atlantic Seafood, The Cultured Mussel
Cookbook, Low Cost Heart Smart Cooking* and
Microwaving Seafood Dinners. She lives in
Prince Edward Island, Canada.

Other Fine Cookbooks from Ragweed Press

The Apple A Day Cookbook
Janet Reeves

In *The Apple A Day Cookbook*, Janet Reeves explores a food of mythic proportions: the Apple. From appetizer to aperitif, salads to sauces, bread and breakfast to the main course meal, this book features the fabled fruit in its many irresistible forms. There are tried-and-true apple recipes from around the world, historical and nutritional facts, illustrations and trivia, and a lively introduction by a descendant of the legendary Johnny Appleseed.

An "apple a day" will never be the same!

ISBN 0-921556-32-2
$13.95

One Potato, Two Potato: A Cookbook and More!
Janet Reeves

Ever try Potato Coconut Fudge? Chocolate-Potato Layer Cake? Or how about Pumpkin-and-Potato Soup? *One Potato, Two Potato: A Cookbook and More!* adds a new twist to an old favourite — the World's #1 Vegetable, the potato. This book is an affectionate chronicle of the persevering spud. It includes historical and nutritional facts, illustrations, trivia, helpful hints, as well as nearly 300 recipes dedicated to the potato. If you ever thought potatoes were boring, this book will change your mind!

ISBN 0-920304-70-2
$13.95

RAGWEED PRESS books can be found in quality bookstores, or individual orders may be sent prepaid to: RAGWEED PRESS, P.O. Box 2023, Charlottetown, Prince Edward Island, Canada, C1A 7N7. Please add postage and handling ($2.45 for the first book and 75 cents for each additional book) to your order. Canadian residents add 7% GST to the total amount. GST registration number R104383120.